Early Retirement— Boon or Bane?

Conservation of Human Resources Series: 14

OTHER VOLUMES IN THE
Conservation of Human Resources Series

Early Retirement — Boon or Bane?

A Study of Three Large Corporations

DEAN W. MORSE and SUSAN H. GRAY

Foreword by Eli Ginzberg

LandMark Studies · ALLANHELD, OSMUN Montclair

ALLANHELD, OSMUN & CO. PUBLISHERS, INC.

Published in the United States of America in 1980
by Allanheld, Osmun & Co. Publishers, Inc.
(A Division of Littlefield, Adams & Co.)
81 Adams Drive, Totowa, New Jersey 07512

Copyright © 1980 Conservation of Human Resources

Second printing, 1982

Library of Congress Cataloging in Publication Data
Morse, Dean.
    Early retirement—boon or bane?

    (Conservation of human resources series; 14)
    Includes bibliographical references.
    1. Retirement—United States—Case studies. I. Gray,
Susan H., joint author. II. Title. III. Series: Con-
servation of human resources series; 14.
HQ1062.M65   305.2′6   79-54970
ISBN 0-916672-44-1

Printed in the United States of America

For the parents of Susan H. Gray,
Ben and Sophie Case

Contents

List of Tables

Foreword

This book presents the results of a three-company study (manufacturing, communications, retailing) of individuals who retired early from positions in middle management, with salaries of between $20,000 and $50,000 in current dollars during their last year's employment. The financing for the project, for which gratified acknowledgment is made, came from the General Electric Foundation and the study was carried out by the Conservation of Human Resources, Columbia University, with Dr. Dean Morse serving as Principal Investigator.

The participating companies drew a sample, according to specifications set out by the Conservation staff, from individuals who had retired (a) within the last three years, (b) about five years ago, and (c) between seven and ten years ago, in order to include a range of postretirement experience in the survey.

The Conservation staff prepared and pretested an elaborate questionnaire designed to elicit as much information as possible about the preretirement and postretirement experiences of the respondents, particularly their employment and the uses of time for other activities: around the house, for recreation and leisure, and in voluntary organizations. The heart of the questionnaire was designed to elicit their anticipations about and their evaluation of the shift from a regular job to retirement status. We also requested in the letter accompanying the questionnaire that the respondents elaborate on any and all aspects of their retirement experience. About one-third of the group did so, thereby adding substantially to the depth of our undertaking. The questionnaire is reproduced in the appendix.

The computer work was carried out for the Conservation project by Philip Sidel, technical director of the Social Science Computer Research Institute at the University of Pittsburgh. Despite the physical separation of the two staffs, the computer assignment was completed on time and with a minimum of difficulty, for which we are deeply gratified.

Dr. Nicholas Perna served as our liaison with the General Electric Foundation. He was helpful at each stage of the investigation and especially when it came to reviewing the draft report. This book is much improved because of his careful reading and penetrating comments.

While it is customary in academic publications to insert a final chapter that summarizes the findings and recommendations, it appeared advisable in the present case to include an outline in the first chapter to provide the reader with a map of the terrain covered by the investigation, on the basis of which he can better decide which subjects are of special interest for him to peruse in depth.

I would like to thank the staffs of the cooperating companies for their constructive assistance; but in consonance with our promise not to divulge the names of the companies and to reinforce our promise of anonymity to the respondents, they must remain unspecified.

I cannot conclude this foreword without noting that it is regrettably, the exception rather than the rule for a foundation, three large companies, a university research group and more than 1,000 businessmen and businesswomen to participate in a cooperative venture such as the one hereafter reported. But if our pool of useful knowledge is to be deepened and comparative and public policies strengthened, more such cooperative ventures must be undertaken. On behalf of my colleagues and myself, I wish to thank all those who made this study possible. Whether, and to what extent, it is viewed to be a success remains for the reader to determine.

Eli Ginzberg
Conservation of Human Resources
Columbia University

Early Retirement —
Boon or Bane?

1

Introduction

The Retirement Activities Study is the result of two interests. One of these might best be labeled curiosity. Retirement is a relatively new social phenomenon: pensions were unknown in the past except to a favored few who, like Dr. Johnson, drew a pension from the Crown but never stopped working. Not only is retirement new, but the phenomenon now called "early retirement" is so novel that little is really known about certain aspects of it. An exception to this lack of knowledge is the early retirement of blue-collar workers, the subject of a major inquiry several years ago by Richard E. Barfield and James N. Morgan.*

But while Barfield and Morgan concentrated upon the early retirement of automobile workers, whose experiences were contrasted with information provided by a national survey carried out in 1966 of some 3,500 families, we have concentrated upon the experiences of middle-level managerial and professional/technical personnel from three large, but in some ways dissimilar, national corporations. One purpose of the study has been simply to investigate a new social process in some depth. Why do managers and professional/technical personnel retire early? What happens to them after they retire? How

*Richard E. Barfield and James N. Morgan, *Early Retirement: The Decision and the Experience and A Second Look* (Ann Arbor, Michigan: Survey Research Center, Institute for Social Research, 1970).

varied are their experiences? Are they satisfied? Surprised? How do they fill their days? What do they think about their own lot? What do they think about their companies and what do they think about national policies?

The other interest that sparked the study is a concern about matters of corporate and public policy. Early retirement is becoming more frequent, since as recent as a generation ago the norm for retirement was age 65. The Social Security Act gave powerful sanction to age 65, and the large numbers of private pension plans that developed thereafter usually accepted age 65 as a norm. In addition, many large corporations began to set 65 as the age of mandatory retirement, even if exceptions were often made. In spite of the powerful institutional rules which set 65 as the retirement age, a steady erosion of that norm has taken place. The labor force participation rates of older age groups have shown a steady and rapid decline since the 1950s. In some well-publicized instances, prominent corporations have developed plans to induce the early retirement of parts of their labor force, particularly engineers. In other less-publicized instances, more indirect, even covert, pressures have been exerted to induce selected individuals to retire early.

Because of the nature of the managerial pyramid and the possible obsolescence of professional and technical skills, early retirement of middle-level managerial and professional/technical personnel has in some cases seemed to offer a solution to such troubling problems as career plateauing, the blockage of promotions or technological lags.

From the point of view of the employee, early retirement has become more tempting. Generous pension offers, unprecedentedly large accumulations of assets, long tenure with a company (so that an individual could say to himself, I have worked long enough, "paid my dues") combined with the new phenomenon of the two-worker family, and other circumstances have fuelled the trend toward early retirement.

But if early retirement has become more common, what of its effects upon the manpower planning of large corporations, upon pension plans and other employee benefit plans?

In the light of the actual trend toward ever earlier retirement, what will be the effect of changes in the law raising the legal age for mandatory retirement to 70? What about the potential effects of the Age Discrimination in Employment Act? Do managerial employees who have often spent many decades of loyal and productive service with a large corporation elect early retirement because the grass is really greener outside, or is it because the corporation has allowed its own pastures to seem (or be) brown for many middle-level managers and professional/technical employees?

Do highly educated, experienced, productive and skilled individuals, retiring when they are still vigorous and can anticipate many more years of life, represent an important under- or unutilized resource which the nation cannot afford to waste? Have plans to retire early been frustrated by unanticipated inflation? Have some "early retirees" found ways to reenter the private sector or found significant and satisfying roles in either the public sector or in nonprofit services? If some of them have, what lessons can be distilled from their experiences that might help others to understand the opportunities and challenges that early retirement offers?

These and other questions, related to actual or potential policy issues of corporations or the public at large, provided both framework and purpose for our investigation. At the same time, we did not want our preconceptions about the nature of the early retirement experience to distort the character of the responses. We tried to make it clear to the respondents that we were just as interested in the nonpaid activities of those who elected early retirement as we were in their work-for-pay activities. The questionnaire instrument, a copy of which is in the appendix, has sections dealing with work activities, voluntary service activities, home maintenance and domestic chores, and recreational activities. In retrospect, and as several respondents pointed out to us, we should have given respondents more opportunity to give details about their voluntary work, in both its quantitative and qualitative aspects.

Respondents were encouraged to add comments, both within the body of the questionnaire and at the end. Many of the respondents who were deeply engaged in volunteer work took advantage of the invitation to add comments to the questionnaire by writing at length about the satisfactions and problems associated with volunteer work.

The following outline presents sequentially the principal characteristics of the respondents, the highlights of their actions in the preretirement years, their postretirement work experience, their income, the extent to which they planned for retirement, their attitudes toward their company, and the implications of the study for corporate and public policy.

Profile of Respondents

Most of the group retired before their 63rd birthdays after an average of 36 years of service with their employers.

More than half of the group had worked for their companies for 36 or
more years; only one in ten for less than 25 years.

Most of the respondents were males and most of them were married at
the time of their response.

Over half of the group had not acquired college degrees. While most
of them had served in managerial capacities before retirement,
those who continued to work after retirement did so overwhelmingly in either professional or technical capacities.

The Preretirement Period

THE EARLY RETIREMENT DECISION

The decision was influenced by one or more of the following elements
in declining order of importance:

Financial ability to retire
Work stress
Reached plateau
Had worked enough
Health
Alternative career opportunities

PLANNING FOR RETIREMENT

The majority had at least a year's foreknowledge about the time when
they would retire.

Most of the prospective retirees had given little or no thought to
postretirement employment of any sort.

Only a small group considered how their retirement might affect
their working spouses.

Most of the group took actions to plan their finances in light of their
upcoming retirements.

Planning for travel and a possible change in residence was also a
prominent part of their preretirement planning activity.

USEFULNESS OF PLANNING

(Assessment by those who thought about it or who took steps to plan)

Planning with respect to finances, residence or travel was found to be
most useful.

Only a minority of those who planned ahead with respect to their postretirement employment (or who considered how their wife's retirement might be coordinated to their own) found their efforts worthwhile.

UTILIZATION OF COMPANY'S COUNSELING SERVICES

Two out of five used the services and of this number most thought that they were "very useful" or "moderately useful."
Of those who did not use the services, more than half reported that the company did not provide any. The remainder thought the counseling would not be useful or did not want to discuss their personal problems with a company employee.

TIMING OF RETIREMENT

Three out of four reported that retirement came at the right time.
One in five reported it came too soon; only 3 percent said it came too late.
For those who said it came too soon, the principal reasons for this judgment in declining order of importance were:
  Inflation
  Miss challenge of work
  Stock market
  Miss contact with people
  Not enough to do

EXPECTATIONS ABOUT RETIREMENT

More than half reported that their retirement experience had been very much what they expected, one-third that it had been "fairly similar" to their expectations.
Among those whose expectations about retirement had not been met, the principal reasons turned out to be lessened income and poor health. Only a small minority enjoyed more income and better health than they had anticipated.

Postretirement Work Experience

WORK EXPERIENCE

A minority worked (two out of five), mostly less than full time. Those with more education, higher incomes, and younger age at retirement were more likely to work after retirement.

Most of those who worked obtained their jobs prior to or shortly after they retired, predominantly with smaller enterprises.

The principal reasons were a liking for work and a desire for additional income.

Most of those who were self-employed or in consulting found their present work more satisfying than their earlier corporate employment.

Most of those who weren't working didn't want to.

Use of Time: Pre- and Postretirement

VOLUNTARY ACTIVITIES

Slightly over half of all respondents participated in voluntary activities, pre- and postretirement, the majority with religious organizations.

In the preretirement period about nine out of ten devoted from 1 to 5 hours a week to voluntary activities. As one might expect, in the postretirement period an even greater proportion of time was spent in voluntary activities.

HOME AND HOBBIES

In their preretirement years, only one out of fourteen respondents spent more than 10 hours a week on home maintenance; after retirement, over one in four spent more than 10 hours on home maintenance. A comparable shift occurred with respect to domestic chores.

An even more radical shift occurred with respect to time devoted to hobbies; after retirement three out of five reported spending more than 10 hours on such activities.

WORK

Prior to retirement most respondents worked between 40 and 45 hours a week; after retirement, those who worked averaged 20 hours of work per week.

Income

Mean preretirement annual earned income in 1977 dollars amounted to $28,800, total family income to $34,500. The $5,700 difference represented an admixture of spouses' earnings and investment income. Mean family income in the 12 months preceding the survey totaled $19,500.

In seven out of ten cases, respondents' preretirement earnings accounted for all of the family's earned income; in the postretirement period only two out of five respondents accounted for all of the family's earned income.

In eight out of ten cases, income from investments accounted for 25 percent or less of preretirement total family income. Postretirement investment income accounted for more than 50 percent of total family income in about one out of five families.

In one out of three families, pensions and social security benefits accounted for more than 75 percent of total postretirement income.

The Planning Mode

The respondents can be subdivided into three groups depending on the importance of planning in their life styles. One group, about one out of ten respondents, could be designated "planners" because they clearly made and revised plans for work and life, not only at retirement but throughout adulthood. At the other extreme, about one out of five respondents were nonplanners who did not think ahead, much less act in anticipation of the future. They took things as they came but only when they came. The third group can best be designated "quasi-planners." They did some thinking in advance and some planning, but not much.

Knowing the date of one's retirement well in advance enabled those who wanted to plan to do so, or at least to have more time to think through what they wanted to do in the future; for the most part this group reported itself more satisfied with retirement than others who improvised. A paradoxical finding emerged, however. Those who did the most detailed planning, on all fronts, reported a discrepancy between what they expected and what they encountered in retirement. The very concreteness of their plans apparently proved a drawback when reality undermined these plans in part, if not in whole. Among the most-satisfied retireees were those who kept themselves open to the future "to go wherever their fancy took them."

Many respondents emphasized that planning for their postretirement income and future work were the two critical aspects of bridging the past and the future. They reported that they could have profited from more assistance with respect to each.

Attitudes Towards the Company

A large number of respondents went out of their way to compliment their former company by such comments as: "best company in the world," "proud to have worked for it," and "fair and honest policies," and even asked the CHR staff to pass on these comments. They indicated a pleasure in participating in a study that involved their company.

There was a small but articulate minority whose views varied from highly critical to hostile—largely because their company, in their view, did not deal decently with the older managerial group. Their comments include: "I was 100 percent loyal until the last year," "the cruel trauma of separation," and "they did not play it straight."

With respect to their pensions, respondents made the following points:

They were grateful for cost-of-living adjustments but felt that they were too small and too infrequent.

They expressed marked resentment at the differences between public and private pension policies, with a COLA (Cost of Living Adjustment) built into Social Security.

They were distressed by the removal of coverage of medical expenses for one's spouse that occurred in the benefit plan of one of the participating companies.

Should pension arrangements (benefits) be improved for current employees, the respondents felt that these changes should be made retroactive so that those who built the company would not be discriminated against.

In the case of one company, postretirement income and assets were heavily dependent upon accumulations of stock in the company rather than upon a defined benefit pension. Many respondents pointed out that this program was generous when it was initiated but that it had been badly eroded by the joint effects of high levels of inflation and declines in the stock market.

Respondents quite often reported favorably on their postretirement contacts with their company—as a way of maintaining their ties—except when communications were pro forma. They wanted to remain a member of the "company family."

The respondents were generally critical of the retirement counseling that had been offered them and considered it too shallow. They stressed the need for such counseling to be made available considerably in advance of the retirement date and the need for expert assistance with respect to finances and health benefits.

A minority of respondents urged companies to institute a tapering-off program for persons approaching retirement, at least two to three years before severance. This would enable the older experienced person to pass on some of his expertise to younger employees. They also recommended that the company develop a roster of the skills of the retirement group with the possibility of recalling them in case of need, a practice which one of the companies had followed, much appreciated by those recalled.

Attitudes Toward National Policies

Most respondents reacted negatively to the change in federal law that enables most individuals to remain at work until they reach 70. Their criticisms referred to the need to make room for younger people, to avoid favoritism, and to give everybody clear-cut information as to when retirement would occur. A minority who took another point of view saw no reason for any mandatory retirement age and believed that most people would taper off at around 65.

Even more pervasive resentment was expressed against the "earnings limitation" under Social Security. This was true even for those who were not working and had no plans to work. The respondents viewed Social Security as a "pension" and believed that older persons should be entitled to keep whatever they earn after they retire. Some pointed out that if they worked, their marginal tax rate would approach or even exceed 100 percent, which they felt was grossly unfair. Others called attention to the dysfunctional aspects of the current tax regulation, since it deprived the nation of the potential contribution of some of the most experienced people.

But the strongest criticisms were reserved for the impact of *inflation* on the retired: comments called attention to the great anxiety and fear caused by continuing high inflation and the conviction that government had neither the will nor the skill to cope with inflation.

On the basis of the foregoing findings the following policy issues have been identified and are briefly discussed under two headings—corporate and public sector. It should be emphasized that the three-company study reflects the attitudes of technical and managerial personnel and that care must be taken not to project the respondents' replies to blue-collar and nonexempt white-collar workers.

Corporate Policy Considerations

1.   The major discordant note of the respondents concerned the difficulties of managing financially in retirement with a set dollar pension during a period of rapid inflation. Many appreciated the fact that their companies had made some unilateral upward adjustment in their pensions but at the same time felt that these adjustments were generally inadequate and favored the currently employed over the retired workers.

In the face of continuing inflation that is likely to yield—if at all— only slowly, what can companies do to mitigate the considerable discontent that will arise from the erosion of pension benefits? It may be possible for some of the stronger companies to provide a COLA for some minimum amount of a variable pension. Opportunity should be offered employees to make voluntary contributions during their years of employment, especially when the needs for current income diminish. By building up a greater equity in their pensions, they will have a partial hedge against erosion from inflation. The last decade has demonstrated that more and more Americans are owners of homes and that such ownership has proved to be a major bulwark against the loss of asset value from inflation. In future corporate approaches to fringe benefit arrangements, the importance of home ownership as an appreciating asset to retirees should be taken into consideration.

Corporate management must contemplate that, if the inflation continues largely unabated, prospective retirees with private pension rights might seek legislation aimed at requiring a COLA in company plans. This possibility should be closely monitored, and alternative proposals, including employee contributions as noted above, should be considered.

A related prospect is legislative intervention aimed at forcing companies to continue contributions to some, if not all, pension and benefit programs, for workers who elect to remain at work past 65. The logic of such intervention is powerful if fringe benefits come to be viewed generally as "deferred earnings."

2.   There is scattered evidence since the three-company study was initiated that many employees who would have retired at 65 have opted to remain at work, reflecting the rise of the "retirement age" to

70. Inflationary erosion of pension benefits must be presumed to be the single most-potent factor leading to the extension of employment. There are signs, including legislative action in several states, suggesting that all ceilings on "forced retirement" may be eliminated.

3. The opportunity that has now been provided by law for most employees who are in good health to remain at work between 65 and 70 and possibly beyond (as some state legislation indicates) carries with it unexplored implications for productivity, promotions and total personnel costs. Corporations would be well advised to review their personnel evaluation systems and make sure that they take appropriate action on employees who in their latter forties or early fifties are no longer working to capacity. Failure to act early may preclude the corporations acting later when administrative agencies and the courts may be on the lookout for discriminatory action based on age.

At a minimum, corporate planning should now be initiated aimed at projecting various scenarios under which 25, 50, or 75 percent of those reaching 65 years of age elect to remain at work. The continuance of high-level inflation is likely to push the figure toward the higher rather than the lower level.

4. The respondents in the three-company study did not, in general, opt for working beyond the retirement age of 65, but there was strong support for the introduction of a system of reduced work schedules as the employee approached retirement that might be continued after he reached 65. To what extent are corporations in a position to experiment with such modified work schedules? Westinghouse introduced it some years ago but apparently did not find it successful. Even if such an approach were fraught with difficulties, it might provide a desirable alternative to a policy that forced a corporation to keep all able-bodied employees in full-time positions until they reached 70 or beyond.

5. There was considerable discontent among the respondents about the inadequacies of the preretirement counseling opportunities available in their companies and about the communications that they received after retirement. The following alternatives suggest themselves. At present it appears that many companies are willing to provide some preretirement services but are reluctant to commit themselves to a wider-ranging program covering postretirement employment, financial management, relocation or more. Many of our respondents were clearly dissatisfied with the quality of counseling support which had been offered them. Among other options,

large corporations have the following: beefing up the programs that they now offer in-house; providing a basic sum to cover preretirement counseling from a reputable external agency; or limiting their involvement to providing information about reliable external agencies. In view of the fact that preretirement counseling involves advice about the management of funds, property, savings and pensions, and since such advice is frequently wrong, corporations might be well advised to avoid becoming entangled in this area or to keep the lowest possible profile.

With respect to communicating with retired workers about the company in general and more specifically about pension arrangements, employers should reassess the information that they currently make available as to frequency, comprehensiveness, ease of understanding, etc. Since there is considerable evidence indicating that retired persons are deeply concerned about the financial base on which their pensions rest, they can use considerable reassurance on this score.

6.   Although inflationary trends plus the raising of the retirement age from 65 to 70 (and future changes that might eliminate the ceiling entirely) suggest a piling-up of workers at the higher ages, two pieces of evidence must be considered that point in the opposite direction. Many of our respondents were pleased with the opportunity to retire as early as 60, and there is considerable confirmatory evidence that many Americans continue to look forward to early retirement. The critical question is whether they will be able to do so without a substantial reduction in their standard of living. On this latter point, employers must take into account that more and more prospective retirees in the future will have wives with private pensions and Social Security entitlements as well as larger financial assets. These factors may compensate, in part if not in whole, for the unsettlement brought about through continuing inflation. Corporate planners will want to keep abreast of the changes in Social Security benefits and private pensions available not only to their own employees but also to their spouses. The determination of an adequate pension must increasingly be based on the family's total financial position.

Public Sector Considerations

1.   Although the majority of respondents opposed the raising of the retirement age from 65 to 70, a minority expressed the view that any retirement based on an arbitrary figure was discriminatory if the

individual were able to continue performing his or her work. The odds favor the removal through legislation of all arbitrary age ceilings in the years ahead, particularly once the swollen inflow of younger people into the labor force declines, as it is scheduled to do by three million in the 1980s, and once the improved health and stamina of many, though not all, older persons, is also recognized (resulting from lessened mortality and an improved standard of living). Employers should consider at this time their stance toward such a legislative challenge.

2.   Closely connected with the above is the beginning of legislative action at both the federal and state levels to mandate or encourage public and private employers to provide a significant number of part-time positions for different groups, particularly married women and older persons. There may be some room for eventual trading between eliminating the age ceiling and providing more part-time jobs.

3.   The most important issue in the public domain with respect to retirement in the years ahead is the future of the Social Security system. Among the more important issues that have surfaced which the corporate world should study with care are the relative strengths and weaknesses of the following proposals:

a) To finance the Social Security system through greater reliance on general tax revenues. Since recent years have demonstrated the limited capacity of the macro-economists to fine-tune the economy, it would probably prove dysfunctional to move in the direction of greater reliance on general revenues. The losses are easily pinpointed, the gains problematic.

b) If the perceived difficulties in financing the Social Security system late in this century and shortly thereafter are reinforced, there may be merit in Secretary Juanita Krep's proposal to move gradually to raise the age qualifications for full benefits from 65 to 68.

c) The experts have demonstrated that the present Social Security system is discriminatory toward working wives (although women are favored by having the option to retire with full benefits at 62). The odds are strong that through judicial opinion or legislation, or both, these discriminations against working wives will sooner or later be eliminated.

d) Some steps have recently been taken to eliminate "double dipping" by federal employees who receive benefits from two federal pension systems, and more constraints are likely to be legislated. The trend, however, is for an increasing number of

older persons to reach retirement age with benefits from multiple private systems or from Social Security and a second governmental system.

e) One of the major challenges to the Social Security system is
the recent rapid rise in disability payments. So far little in the
way of corrective action has been instituted. The corporate
world might well devote some resources to probing the causes
for this increase and how it might be brought under control.

Our respondents indicated a considerable unease about the future
of the Social Security system at the same time that they found it
commendable that Social Security payments are indexed, which is
not true for private pensions. Their most bitter complaint was against
the loss of benefits once their earnings reached the earned income
ceiling.

In sum, public policy will have to weigh the prospects of older
Americans working longer, at least to 68, or accepting higher taxes on
workers and taxpayers to support the Social Security system. If
private pensions cannot be indexed, employees may seek a greater
part of their total retirement income from public sources. An
alternative modification would be to enable older workers to earn
more before suffering a diminution in their benefits. Unless the
public is willing to contemplate substantial additional costs, some
restraints will have to be placed on the steep rise in disability
payments, although the methods for accomplishing this are far from
clear. It is likely that the courts will force the elimination of sex
discrimination against women, if Congress should fail to act, which
will further increase the costs.

To conclude the implications for public policy, the three-legged
stool to provide income for older persons through Social Security,
private pensions, and personal assets still dominates the U.S. environment; but the continuance of substantial inflation over a period of
years is certain to force hard choices that will alter, if not funda-
mentally change, the approach that the nation has been following
since World War II, which has seen a vast reduction in poverty among
older persons.

In the following chapters, the large corporations from which the
respondents came are identified as the Manufacturer, the Chain Store,
and the Utility. We have followed a fairly straightforward path in
presenting the results of the Retirement Activities Study. Chapter 2
deals with the retirement decision itself, its background, the degree of

planning associated with the retirement decision, and the degree of counseling (or lack of counseling) that was associated with the decision. Chapter 3 is devoted to work activity after retirement, the reasons for working and the character of the work activity itself. Approximately two-fifths of the respondents performed some work during the years of their retirement, and about three in ten were actually working at the time of the survey or had worked at some time during the previous 12 months. In addition, a large proportion, more than a quarter of the respondents, not at work at the time of the survey, indicated some interest in work in the future. The reasons for their not working are examined.

Chapter 4 turns to the nonpaid activities of the respondents. It explores voluntary service activity, work around and for the home, and a wide range of recreational activities. Chapter 5 presents differences and commonalites among important subgroups of the respondents, particularly the contrast between the experiences of the respondents who retired early in the period covered by the investigation, 1968-1977, compared to those who retired more recently. It also examines the experiences of the female respondents, admittedly a small number but for that reason a pioneering group.

In Chapter 6 we have presented a distillation of the comments of the more than one-third of the respondents on a wide range of subjects. Since the respondents were encouraged to comment upon several specific policy issues, both corporate and public, much of the chapter is devoted to the suggestions and reflections of respondents about these issues. We have made an effort to select comments that were representative of respondents' views.

Our understanding of the character of the early retirement experience, its satisfactions and its disappointments, was very much influenced by the generous comments made by many of the respondents. In several instances we would have liked to present much longer comments, but space limitations have restricted us to the sample offered in this chapter.

Finally, Chapter 7 gives our own views, which we hope reflect adequately what we have learned from our respondents, both from their answers to specific questions of the survey instrument and from their written comments, about a number of policy issues. We have in this chapter also presented a framework for identifying potential policy issues. The most important of these issues have already been discussed in the outline in this introductory chapter. In Chapter 7 we have taken the opportunity to comment further upon some of these issues.

2

The Retirement Decision

The decision to retire was based upon many factors. Not all of our respondents made that decision themselves. About one-quarter had reached the mandatory age for their level within their company and had little choice.

Another 5 percent said that they had been forced out, for example by corporate shifts, reductions in personnel or interpersonal conflicts with superiors. These persons felt interpersonal conflicts and/or corporate structural reorganizations made early retirement a more comfortable option than remaining in an untenable work situation. One respondent, for example, a male Manufacturing retiree, presently not working for pay, who spent 30 years in engineering before retiring in 1977 at the age of 62 with a family income of $12,000, blamed the ethnic composition of a new management crew for forcing his decision to retire early:

I had not planned early retirement, as my job was exciting, challenging, and management at that point in time was excellent. However a complete change in management occurred in 1975. (#293)

Another, a male Utility retiree who worked 37 years before retiring in 1977 at the age of 59, presently not working for pay and with a present family income of $10,000, placed the blame on attempted employee attrition:

I feel my company needed to reduce the employees and did everything they could to force my retirement. If I didn't have the years of service, so I was able to retire, I would have worked under a very hard time. However, what I have seen and heard in the past years, this is the way business is operating.

I am very glad I was financially secure to retire at the age of 59 and not have to work under the present attitude of management. (#483)

The rest of our respondents initiated their own early retirement, often for several reasons. The most common reasons for doing so were monetary; either they had accumulated enough assets, were attracted by the pension, or had calcuated that after taxes, the financial incentive to continue working was no longer sufficiently high when compared to the pension. Eighty-eight percent of the retirees in our sample who initiated their early retirement indicated finances were one of the reasons for deciding to retire.* One typical respondent, a 70-year-old male Manufacturing retiree who retired in 1969 after 43 years in production, with a present family income of $32,000, wrote:

Throughout my working life I looked forward to the day when I could shed the discipline of a steady job, and be my own boss at last. I never aspired to amass a fortune. When I was assured of sufficient income for my family's modest basic needs, I retired and proceeded at last to do some of the things I had always wanted to do, rather than those which other people demanded. I now spend more time with my family. I enjoy traveling, writing and other hobbies, and puttering around the house and garden.

So far I have no regrets. I have been fortunate in qualifying for two retirement pensions—one from the Army and one from my company. Otherwise I would not be quite so free of apprehension for the future and the eroding effects of worsening inflation. (#42)

Health factors and the stresses and physical demands of their jobs also played a large role in the decision to retire early. Fifty-eight percent of early retirees also mentioned these as reasons. A male Utility retiree presently not working for pay who retired last year at the age of 60 after 36 years in cost accounting, with a family income of $22,000, wrote:

*Respondents often checked more than one reason for deciding to retire.

I was retired because of a serious heart condition, that coupled
with the fact that I was reporting to a "supervisor" who has a
definite psychological problem besides being a plain S.O.B.
Therefore it was to my best interest to retire after my year of
disability terminated. (#795)

Even so, about a quarter of those who had retired early because of
health considerations, among other reasons, subsequently began
working again, a relatively high proportion in consulting work or
self-employment where, perhaps, the stresses and strains of work were
reduced from their preretirement level.

Tied into these reasons were other negative feelings about continuing to work in general, or, specifically, about their own jobs. Thirty-
one percent of early retirees said they no longer liked their work and
the same percentage said they felt they had worked long enough, as in
this comment from a 69-year-old male Manufacturing retiree with a
present family income of $11,000. He had spent 39 years in sales and
marketing.

I had no objections whatever to retirement at 65, in fact I
welcomed it. I was offered consulting work after retirement but
rejected it, and in retrospect am most happy I did. I spend from
May 1 to Sept 31 in my Adirondack mountain camp and lead a
thoroughly unregimented and somewhat irresponsible life. I
feel I have paid my dues. (#23)

Respondents who had requested early retirement were also asked
whether discontent with a job, taking either the form of lack of
challenge and satisfaction due to having "risen as far as I could" or
because of working "under supervision" or because of "conflict with
my superiors" were among the circumstances leading to their request
for early retirement. A surprisingly large proportion, about a third of
the early retirees, indicated that "having risen as far as I could" with
the associated lack of challenge and satisfaction of their job was
among the factors leading to their retirement request. This was
particularly characteristic with Utility retirees. One male Utility
retiree who worked as a consultant for 40 years before retiring at the
age of 61 in 1975, with a present family income of $10,000, writes:

It seems as one grows older, the mental fatigue associated with
your job affects your physical willingness to do things after you
get home from a typical day at your job. I suppose the main
reason I retired was to break the monotony of getting up at 5:30

every morning and returning at 6 p.m. or after for 40 years, even though my job was very satisfying without, what is called, excessive pressure.

If a business could be arranged to have its employees stagger their hours *once in a while* I think many benefits would be enjoyed by the employer. (#612)

A much smaller proportion indicated that discontent with working under a supervisor (one out of ten) or direct conflict with superiors (one out of seven) had brought about their retirement request.

Finances which were adequate to make retirement possible acted in conjunction with negative aspects of preretirement jobs. Obviously, if a job were still highly attractive, having enough assets to retire might not be as strong a spur toward retirement as it would be if a job were tedious, stressful or otherwise unattractive. Similarly, no matter how attractive early retirement might otherwise seem, a lack of adequate financing would tend to discourage it to some extent. Very few retirees had retired early specifically to do other types of work or to work for a different employer. The choice for most was either to remain where they were or to withdraw themselves to a large extent from the labor market, although a permanent withdrawal was not ultimately the outcome for a substantial proportion of them.

Some retirees, however, who did not have enough assets to retire but eagerly wanted to, made the choices of either getting by with a lot less or planning for some kind of postretirement work. Forty-three percent of those retirees who initiated their retirement but at the time of retirement did not feel that they had sufficient assets subsequently had some kind of work experience, compared to 29 percent of the group with sufficient assets.

Among the possible reasons for an individual's initiating a request for retirement is of course an offer of employment by another company. It is interesting to note that practically none of those respondents who initiated a retirement request did so because another company had offered them employment. In some cases, it is true, individuals had made arrangements for postretirement salaried employment before they retired, but this seems to have been much more on their own initiative. Only 18 respondents indicated that their retirement was associated with an offer of employment by another company. But another 70 respondents made arrangements for a job before they retired.

Another relatively small group of respondents, 50 in number, indicated that they had requested retirement because "the time was opportune . . . to engage in consulting work or self-employment." The proportion giving this reason was highest in the Utility company. The actual work experience of this group during retirement confirmed to a very high degree that their planning was geared to reality. More than 90 percent of this group had postretirement work experience, and almost all of their work experience took the form of self-employment and/or consulting work.

There was a relationship in general between the method of exiting from one's preretirement job and subsequent labor market participation. Those who initiated their request for retirement were somewhat more likely to be subsequently working for pay. One reason for this was that they were a generally younger age group than those who had reached mandatory retirement age. Not only are the opportunities for a younger age group greater, but a longer projected life span and younger dependents coupled with the present inflationary trend would also encourage postretirement work for pay. This group was twice as likely to have been consultants at some time during their retirement (about one in seven compared to less than one in 14). Those respondents whose retirement was involuntary but not occasioned by their attaining mandatory retirement age were the most likely to work after retirement, particularly in self-employment.

Attitudes Toward the Timing of Retirement

In looking backward to make an evaluation about the correctness of the timing of their retirement, what had happened subsequently played a large role. Most retirees (75 percent) felt that they had retired at about the right time. Of the 22 percent* who felt that their timing was off, however, most (19 percent) felt that they had retired too soon rather than too late. Common reasons for feeling that retirement had occurred too soon were financial. Sixty-nine percent felt that inflation had eroded the value of their income. Those dependent upon stock market investments also had experienced an adverse effect upon their net worth, causing them to worry about a lowering of their standard of living (53 percent). Chain Store retirees were more likely to feel that they retired too soon than retirees in the other two corporations. Chain Store retirees were those most likely to be affected

*3 percent did not respond.

by adverse conditions in the stock market, since a substantial part of their postretirement incomes was generally tied to Chain Store stock.

At the time of their retirement, a good proportion of the Chain Store retirees could have correctly perceived that they had very considerable assets in the form of company stock and that these assets would provide a solid basis for a comfortable retirement income. Although middle-level managers and technical/professional staff of the other two companies had also been encouraged to accumulate assets in the form of company stock, their retirement benefits were primarily based upon defined benefit pensions.

A substantial number of those who retired too soon also missed either the challenge of their jobs (63 percent) or the contact they had previously had with people on their jobs (47 percent). Very few retirees who felt they had retired too soon complained that they presently did not have enough to do (18 percent).

Financial setbacks and positive feelings about their former careers were incentives which made this group more likely to be working for pay than other retirees. Forty-two percent were working for pay compared to about a fourth of other retirees. Disappointments with subsequent work opportunities compared to prior careers and financial complaints would lead to the feeling that retirement had been inopportune, whereas retirees who had made better retirement adjustments saw their retirement timing as more correct. For example, a third of those who felt they had retired too soon and were not working gave the lack of opportunities in their field as a reason, compared to 9 percent of those who felt their timing had been about right. Similarly, less than a quarter of those not working for pay who indicated that they had retired too soon said they did not want to work, compared to almost two-thirds of other retirees.

Attitudes toward the timing of retirement were also related to feelings about health status since retirement. Those who felt they retired too soon also believed their health had suffered since retirement, whereas those who thought that their health had improved were more likely to say that they had retired too late. Those who had been more resistant to retirement might have had their health or perceived health adversely affected by the strains of coercive retirement. It is also possible and probable, however, that the judgment concerning the timing of retirement was made retrospectively in light of the health outcome.

Most of those who thought they had retired too late were enjoying the freedom from job-related pressures and wished that they had freed themselves sooner.

It is important that *no one* who felt he had retired too late indicated that if he had retired earlier, he would have been able to secure better postretirement work.

Planning for Retirement

There were three types of planners: those who planned carefully, those who did some degree of planning and those who made little or no plans for retirement. Some careful planners started on their own to plan in advance for their retirement years. A male Utility retiree, presently not working for pay with a current family income of $15,000, was a model planner. He retired in 1969 at the age of 65 after 39 years in industrial engineering:

Having observed many retired persons, I noticed that those who had made no plans for their retirement acted like lost sheep. Therefore, at age 43, I asked myself what I would do with my time when I retired. Decided on the following activities:

Summer	*Winter*
Gardening	Greenhouse
Painting	*Model railroading
Photography	Woodworking
	Stamp collecting
	Reading

There is considerable overlap in the seasons. Now recognizing that income would probably be reduced at retirement, bought a ten-acre estate in 1949 and ten years later owned it free and clear. During the last three years before retirement collected and paid for items to be used primarily after retirement. Bought and paid for woodworking equipment (12" radial arm saw and complete line of accessories, drill press, etc.). Built a plastic greenhouse to see if I would enjoy winter indoor gardening.

This allowed me to have almost all the things needed to keep me well occupied and not have to spend any appreciable amount of retirement income.

My expenses are mainly for food, heat, electric, phone, car upkeep and taxes. This, for me, because of the planning has resulted in a most pleasurable retirement. (#796)

---

*Not running trains! Involves carpentry, electrical and electronic work, preparing layouts, laying track, landscaping, painting, and building from scratch such items as cars, houses and industrial buildings.

Others such as this male Utility retiree did hardly any planning at all. Presently not working for pay, with a current family income of $15,000, he retired in 1969 at the age of 65 after 46 years in maintenance. He reports:

During the year before retirement my wife and I made some tentative plans. Florida, we agreed, was not considered because, first, we did not want to be that far away from our children and grandchildren, and also because we had purchased a modest summer home near the ocean in southern New Jersey. This also ruled out extensive travel. [Cites friends' experiences with plans that did not work out.] This was when we stopped making detailed plans. We decided to "play it by ear" for one year and see how things were going. Nine years later we are still in the same key and love it. (#654)

Most retirees knew at least their retirement date in advance, even if little other advance planning was done. Fifty-three percent knew their retirement date more than a year before retirement, and 35 percent knew in the year before retirement. Only 10 percent had little advance warning.*

The further in advance that persons knew their retirement date, the more likely they were to plan, with the exception of retirees who were model planners and tended to plan ahead in all areas, regardless of when retirement would be. Knowing one's retirement date well in advance also increased the likelihood of satisfaction with retirement and the probability that one's experiences would be close to what was expected, although not necessarily because of the greater opportunity to plan.

In actuality, complete planners are less likely to find retirement to be what they expected and are more likely to qualify their retirement satisfaction than those who make little or no plans. Because they have sketched out in their minds a clearer idea of what retirement is to be like and because their expectations are more concrete, there is more room for their conceptions to be negated, causing some dissatisfaction, than there is for the person who has only vague conceptions concerning what awaits him at retirement.

Greater planning led to higher satisfaction and a sharper alignment of preretirement expectations with postretirement reality in the area of investments and travel. With other areas of preretirement

*Two percent did not answer this question.

planning, there were too many factors beside extent of planning which could influence outcome and satisfaction.

Few people were model planners or did not planning at all. Most retirees either thought about or took concrete steps to plan for at least three of the following possible aspects of retirement: salaried employment after retirement, self-employment or consulting work, their spouse's retirement, postretirement income from investments, travel, and a change of residence. The most common areas in which planning took place were postretirement investments, travel, and a change of residence. Nine percent planned to move to a retirement community and 23 percent planned to move to the sunbelt. Planning for specific aspects of retirement appeared to have been most useful in the areas where concrete steps were actually taken, rather than only considered.

Those who had taken concrete steps to plan for salaried employment after retirement were presently more likely to be working for pay and to be employed. Similarly, those who took steps to plan for self-employment or consulting were also more likely to be performing those activities. Some 183 respondents indicated that they had taken active steps either to secure employment, or to engage in consulting or self-employment, or both. Another 387 respondents had either thought about employment or consulting and self-employment or both. In sum then, one-half of our respondents were interested enough in the prospect of working after retirement either to take active steps to secure work or to think about it in a planning sense.

Not surprisingly, those who planned to travel or to move to a retirement community or the sunbelt were less likely to be working for pay. It is of interest, however, that even in retirement communities, 24 percent of retirees who had relocated there were working for pay. In the sunbelt area, the figure was 32 percent.

Planning and Inflation

The severity of current inflation was a factor that many respondents had not planned for. A male Manufacturing retiree, presently not working for pay, who retired in 1971 at the age of 60 after 30 years in production with a present family income of $9,000-10,000, complained:

The Savings and Security plan had delivered to me a very substantial and comforting financial buffer. I used part of it to liquidate all open accounts, to purchase a new car and to pay off the small unpaid balance of my home mortgage. My wife and I continued to live comfortably by drawing from our "buffer" to augment my pension payments.

The best-laid plans of mice and men oft go astray. During the past two or three years, that old devil "inflation" and unheard of increases in local property taxes have drained the balance of our once-substantial buffer. We cannot afford to live in our home any longer, in the home that we worked so hard and so long for. We must sell it this year and move, using the sale price to establish another financial buffer, which hopefully will carry us through the balance of our lives. (#167)

Those who had underestimated the inflation rate were also those least likely to have planned to or to presently be working for pay, thus increasing their financial burden. Over a third of our respondents admitted that at the time of retirement they had not thought much about the average rate of inflation during the rest of their lifetime. Of those who had thought about inflation, 48 percent had also severely underestimated its rate, predicting the average rate to be under 5 percent. Those who had not given much thought to inflation were also those retirees less likely to plan in general.

Company-Provided Counseling and Retirement Planning

Retirement counseling through the retiree's company was one potential vehicle for the reduction of strains, both financial and otherwise, resulting from poor planning. It appears that for our sample, however, this resource has not yet fulfilled its potential. Most respondents did not use company-provided counseling to do their planning (60 percent). One reason for this was lack of information about the services available: more than half of those who did not use company counseling were ignorant of the counseling services available through their companies. The most common reason for not using them is that they thought that the companies involved did not provide them, when in fact they did. Twenty-five percent of those who did not use company counseling knew that their company provided it, but did not think it would be useful. Another 19 percent indicated that they knew that their company provided counseling, but they did not wish to discuss their personal situation with retirement counselors provided by the company.

There were company differences in the use of company-provided services. Chain Store retirees were most likely to use company counseling, Utility retirees the least likely. Chain Store retirees were also those who had the most complaints about company-provided retirement counseling. Although most of those who used these services found them at least somewhat useful (87 percent of those who used them), they were seen to be much in need of improvement. For one thing, literature packets or brochures were viewed as inadequate. Rather, a personal touch was seen to be necessary, as in the following suggestion by a male Chain Store retiree, presently not working, with a current family income of $20,000. He retired in 1977 at the age of 59 after 37 years in distribution and service:

I suggest that planning for retirement should start with the company . . . taking a more precise, a more personal, and a more programmed effort than that presently in practice.

Today's potential retiree is guided by local unit management that is basically untrained for the effort and guidance needed.

I was in the position of attempting to guide the person nearing retirement, and whatever counsel and guidance I provided was for the most part a result of investigative effort on my own.

A professional program originating at the top and imparted to field management is needed at this time, in addition to the written material that is presented to the future retiree for his/her guidance.

In addition to better-trained unit management, it also would seem appropriate for the program to provide "retirement type meetings" at specified locations for meaningful presentations of the many phases of retirement planning—with a personal touch. (#112)

It was believed that other information and help was needed in addition to counseling about company benefits. One respondent, a male Manufacturing retiree currently engaged in consulting, suggested that the company could pay the tuition to counseling courses offered at local colleges:

I think they should offer preretirement counseling (other than just explanations of company benefits). Perhaps pay the tuition to such courses and seminars offered at local colleges. (#199)

The need for expert advice was also stressed, as in this suggestion by a male Chain Store retiree, presently not working. He retired in 1974 at the age of 60 after 29 years in sales and marketing and has a current family income of $12,000:

Chain Store did not have a counseling program in 1974. They did not have a Pension Plan as such. At the end of 30 years I was given a block of company stock. That dropped 60 percent the first six months. Before the market went down it was only paying 2½% in dividends. I think any large company can well afford to have an expert sit down and talk to an employee for an hour or a day and give him different options. (#664)

Expectations and Reality

Most persons were not overly surprised by their retirement experiences. Eighty-four percent said it was at least fairly similar to what they expected. Surprises tended to be in the areas of inflation, as mentioned previously, and adverse health. Those who found retirement very much what they expected were also likely to be very satisfied with it. When finances were unexpectedly affected adversely, the retiree was more likely to return to working for pay. Those who found retirement very much what they expected presumably were most likely to have adequate financial resources and planned alternative uses for their time. Although postretirement employment and self-employment were related to surprises in the area of finances, consulting was not. This indicates that retirees enter the consulting field for a wider variety of reasons than simply an unexpected financial setback, perhaps in order to continue to feel useful in an area directly related to their preretirement career. This might be more possible for retirees through consulting than either working for an employer or setting oneself up in self-employment.

The following male Manufacturing retiree, for example, who retired last year after 25 years in research and development at the age of 55 with a family income of $7,500 and is presently considering returing to work as a part-time consultant explains:

Have been asked to return as a consultant by my past management, which I may do, part time only, only because it's forcing them to admit how valuable I was to them, *which they were very reluctant to do*. Money isn't the only answer to life's satisfaction. (#146)

Attitudes concerning what constituted a sufficient postretirement income varied. Unmet expectations were not related to present total family income nor were they related to the standard of living the retiree was used to before retirement. There was no relationship between whether or not expectations were met and the amount of a person's annual salary in the year before retirement. Chain Store retirees who found their income severely deflated with adverse conditions in the stock market were, not surprisingly, more likely to say that retirement did not meet their expectations and more likely to be dissatisfied.

Adverse health also decreased satisfaction. Only 48 percent of those whose health had gotten worse since retirement said they were satisfied compared to 75 percent of those whose health had improved. Worsening health with age, however, is often expected, whereas financial setbacks might not have been. This may account for why almost half of those with worsening health were still very satisfied.

Satisfaction with retirement was also dependent upon becoming accustomed to differing patterns of behavior. Those who had allocated a smaller number of hours before retirement to both work and nonwork recreational and hobby-type activities were more likely to be very satisfied after retirement, as they were used to a pattern of low time use or perhaps using time in alternate patterns, such as increasing their social activities. Those whose social life had improved since retirement, for example, were more likely to say that their expectations had been met and that they were very satisfied.

The following two cases, one of a retiree who planned for postretirement employment but made no other plans at all, and the other who planned a bit more fully, are examples of some of the planning patterns which emerge and their alignment with reality.

John Alfred is an example of a retiree who is very satisfied and whose expectations for retirement have been met. He worked for 34 years for the Manufacturing corporation in employee relations before retiring in 1970 at the age of 61. He presently earns $12,000 a year working as a teacher:

I had planned for many years prior to retirement to take an early optional retirement in order to teach. For many years—about 30—I had done part-time teaching in the field of adult education. I was interested in full-time "day school" teaching for a few years. (#200)

Mr. Alfred spends 15 hours a week at this job and finds it as satisfying as his previous career. He made the arrangement for this job before he retired, having found his preretirement job decreasing in challenge. He also reported difficulty in living up to performance expectations. He had enough assets to handle the decrease in income occasioned by his retirement and therefore decided to initiate his retirement early, making his plans more than a year in advance. Although his social life is presently less active, his health is about the same and he feels he retired at about the right time.

Steve Warrenkey, on the other hand, is only moderately satisfied with retirement, although he finds his experiences fairly similar to what he expected. He worked for 30 years for Chain Store in sales and marketing before retiring in 1976 at the age of 59. Like Mr. Alfred, he also earns $12,000 a year and is self-employed.

My decision to take early retirement was based primarily on work pressures, lack of a feeling of satisfaction and a feeling that my assets were adequate.

My greatest disappointment has been the stock market performance over the past two years, on which Chain Store retirees depended at that time, the income tax bite and the capital gains treatment change. While Chain Store has changed their retirement policy beginning with 1978, it does not benefit prior retirees.

Federal regulations are only token in their relief for retirees in my situation in the area of taxes, and inflation controls are non-existent.

In short, I couldn't have retired at a worse time! (#290)

Aside from his financial complaints, he also feels his self-employment is less satisfying than his preretirement career, but feels that he needs the income and therefore spends 35 hours per week at his new work. Although he had thought about self-employment before retiring, he had not taken any concrete steps. Like Mr. Alfred he initiated his own retirement, but unlike Mr. Alfred, the time between the decision and the actual retirement was less than a year. Although his health and his social life have both improved since retirement, Mr. Warrenkey believes that he retired too soon.

3

To Work or Not to Work?

Introduction

The great majority of our respondents had worked for at least three decades for their company before they retired, a considerable fraction (one-third) four decades or more. In general, they can be said to have had substantial careers and to have moved upwards in their firm's hierarchy of managerial, technical and professional ranks. Many respondents took the trouble to write that they had enjoyed their long associations with their companies and that they had retired after productive and satisfying careers. With work experience so central to the lives of many of the respondents, what did they do about work in their retirement years?

The first thing to be said is that many of them, more than a majority, found that they could get along without work quite well. On the other hand, a substantial minority found that they wanted to continue working, if only part time and part year. Others found that they were forced to continue working. Overall, about two-fifths of our respondents have had some kind of work experience during their retirement years. In another part of the chapter, we will discuss the experiences and attitudes of respondents who answered "not to work" to the question heading this chapter. Here we will look at those who chose to work or were forced to work.

Summary statistics mask the diversity of human behavior, smooth its rough edges, obscure the vital spark of emotion and intelligence that is at the heart of human choice and action. Since the conventional view of retirement is that an individual ceases to work completely (becomes a "pensioner"), those respondents who continued to work or resumed work at some time during their retirement represent in some ways a socially aberrant group. But since this group contained almost two-fifths of our respondents, it is evident that the conventional norm of "complete retirement" is much honored in the breach. Among this group of middle-level managers, technical and professional personnel, the individual who chose to work after retirement did not have to consider himself or herself deviant. Nevertheless, there is a sense in which he or she did act somewhat at variance with the mainstream.

This variance is revealed, moreover, by the very diversity of new careers and occupations that this group of postretirement workers have followed. The following list—by no means exhaustive—suggests the very wide range of work activity that opened up to our respondents after retirement:

male nurse (he says that he is much in demand)
stock broker
manager of miniature golf courses (having a wonderful time)
economist
cabinet maker (he did this as a youth and now has set up a shop)
president of a 32-unit condominium development
started five churches
teacher ("my raison d'être")
scientific consultant (he built lab and has presented many
    technical papers)
rancher (more than one respondent)
managers of (1) family catering business (2) family-owned small
    bakery
commercial fisherman (two respondents)
restorer of antiques
farmer (several respondents, including a tree farmer and a
    nursery man)
hotel manager (always wanted to be one)
psychologist (teaches gerontology in university, advises retirees)
artist
director of senior citizen center
dance teacher (having a wonderful time)
real estate agents
priest

At least one of our respondents became a "merchant chief" during his retirement. A number of respondents indicated that one of the chief satisfactions of retirement was that it allowed them to take up an occupation or career that they had always wanted to engage in. Often these new careers involved skilled craft work of one kind or another. In other instances, the occupation permitted a much wider range of social contact than work experience before retirement had afforded.

In some cases, the new career gave the respondent an opportunity to use talents and energies which his previous work had not fully explored. The accounts given by some respondents of their postretirement careers have something of a Horatio Alger quality, even though they are told by (and about) managers and technical/professional personnel after they had supposedly completed their lengthy and usually quite successful careers with a large corporation. Here are a few of their experiences.

James Newton retired in 1975 at age 62 from the Chain Store company. His salary was $30,000. He retired because he believed he had enough assets to make retirement possible, because he felt that he had risen as far as he could within the Chain Store and therefore his job no longer provided the same challenge and satisfaction, and because, after 37 years with Chain Store, he felt he had worked long enough for the company. But according to Mr. Newton, there was another reason for retiring at age 62. He had received an attractive offer from another employer. Now, three years later, he is working 40 hours a week year-round for this new employer, a medium-sized firm. His job with Chain Store had been primarily of a professional technical character. His new employer uses him in a managerial capacity. His present work is much more satisfying than the work he had performed for Chain Store.

When asked why he retired only to go back to work, Mr. Newton says that a combination of circumstances determined his decision to continue working. First, taking everything into account, he likes to work. Secondly, he believes that not working might have an adverse effect upon his health. Finally, he was very concerned that continued high rates of inflation might have a disastrous effect upon his future standard of living. After three years with his new employer, Mr. Newton is earning over $50,000 a year, and his total family income has risen from $60,000 a year in 1975 to over $100,000 in 1978. He is very satisfied with retirement from Chain Store. He sums up his experience:

My experience has been most rewarding, spiritually, socially, and financially. It uncovered talents and ability that were never challenged by my preretirement job. (#2)

Robert Manning reached the mandatory retirement age of 65 at the Manufacturing company in 1973. He had been employed in a managerial capacity in one of its research and development departments. He had worked for more than 30 years for the company and did not look forward to his retirement. As he says, "Not that I feared retirement, it was just that I have always lived a highly active life and I just could not picture myself retiring to the life of a country gentleman."

After retirement, Mr. Manning tried to adjust to what he terms "that leisure life," but he found it increasingly difficult to cope with so much free time:

Just how much time can one devote to chores around the house? I read more books in my 10-month retirement than I ever had before. My hobby of woodworking, woodcarving, soon took on the appearance of a full-time job. In fact, the pleasure of doing these things as a means of relaxation soon turned into an 8- to 10-hour job. By this time I had decided to again become actively employed—but not at just anything. It had to be at something that I felt would be useful. (#310)

Mr. Manning thinks he was lucky. Fortunately for him, a new program for the elderly was being developed in his area, a manufacturing center in one of the New England states. He applied for a position and was hired as one of the center's administrators. He now works full time for the entire year and has held this position for almost four years. Unlike Mr. Newton, his salary is much less than it had been when he was employed at Manufacturing, but like Mr. Newton, his work is much more satisfying than the work he was doing before retirement. It is, he says, "One of the most satisfying positions he has ever had," and it keeps him far busier than the 37.5 hours he is officially working. The agency is rather small, but he is involved in many different areas of public service.

Having worked for one of the largest of American corporations before retirement, Mr. Manning particularly enjoys the small scale of operations in his new profession and the "real person-to-person form of satisfaction" his new career provides. Looking back at his retirement, however, he still feels that he retired too soon. In particular he feels that after his retirement he missed the "challenge and excitement involved in performing successfully on my job." But he is also very much influenced by the fact that inflation is eroding the value of his income. Like Mr. Newton, he went back to work, he feels, because he liked to work; he was concerned about the possibility that not working would be bad for his health, and because he feared that inflation might have a calamitous effect upon his standard of living. But he is clear in his mind that the most important of these factors was his concern about health.

Henry Jukes retired from the Utility eight years before mandatory retirement age because a combination of respiratory and cardiac problems, compounded, he believes, by pressures of his work, made retirement imperative. He is a college graduate and had worked almost 30 years for Utility when he retired. His last position with the company was as a manager, and he earned about $25,000 a year. He felt that he had risen as far as he could in the managerial ranks, but that the physical demands of his work were becoming intolerable. As he puts it, "Continuing to work at my job would have caused my health to deteriorate to the point where I could not have been able to pursue my planned activities for retirement."

Like Mr. Newton and Mr. Manning, Henry Jukes is happier in his work now than he was before he retired from "Utility." He is, he reports, "Finally able to do something I enjoy." But Mr. Jukes is not working for an employer and his earnings, so far, are only nominal. He is eloquent about his new career, made possible for him by the liberal retirement benefits provided by "Utility.":

Retirement made possible my engaging in commercial fishing, which I truly enjoy, in an environment which has been most beneficial to my health and has brought to me a new vigor and contentment I had never known in my regular job. I would not recommend retirement for someone who doesn't have an activity to take up to replace their regular job. In my case I find it hard to understand some of my fellow retirees' complaints that they have nothing to do. I do believe that over the course of a career a person can get so involved in a job that they work themselves into the position of being lost without it. Competition for advancement can create this. (#953)

Mr. Jukes, perhaps because of the unusual nature of his postretirement career, has strong feelings about the limitations placed by Social Security on earned income. According to him:

I don't feel the fear of the lack of opportunity for advancement for younger people is a justifiable argument for placing such restrictions. I don't feel that those who have made a decision to retire will attempt to supplement their retirement with a type of job that most younger people would be willing to work at for any period of time.

Frederick Bing retired from Chain Store in 1974 in order to form a corporation with a friend. He was 58 years old when he retired and his salary was $28,500. He had always wanted to be self-employed because, as he puts it, he will be able to work as many more years as he chooses and because he can earn more by being self-employed than by working for an employer. But even Mr. Bing could not have anticipated how much more he could earn. In 1977 he earned $200,000 and is now, with his partner, thinking seriously about starting another business, related to his present business. He sums up his feelings about his retirement:

I have been extremely happy with my postretirement venture which has been *very* successful. I am now 62 years of age and enjoy the challenge of operating a business. If my health continues as it has been, I have no desire to "retire" from my present business. (#418)

Mr. Bing had worked approximately 50 hours a week for Chain Store. He now works close to 60 hours a week at his business. He is able to spend more time at work because he now does very little home-maintenance work. Before retirement, he had spent close to 20 hours a week maintaining his home. But Mr. Bing has no regrets about the increased hours of work he puts in. Compared to his preretirement job, his present work is much more satisfying. And, he does not need to add, much more rewarding economically. His total income was much higher than any of the other respondents. Great economic success may have come late in his life, but perhaps for that reason it seems to be particularly satisfying.

A postretirement business venture does not need to furnish a man with a large income in order to be satisfying. A retired Manufacturing company engineer, Geoffrey Allen, moved from Boston to San Diego to become president and accountant of Bagley's Bakery and Restaurant. He works a modest number of hours as president and this without pay. Bagley's is owned by his daughter, his son-in-law, his wife and himself. It is a small bakery, producing a wide variety of unusual breads, some 25 different kinds in all. Mr. Allen says that he really cannot say whether his present work is more enjoyable than what he did for Manufacturing Company because, as he puts it, "I thoroughly enjoyed my work, especially the last ten years. I am proud to have been a Manufacturing man." The work he now does is entirely different. But it has unusual rewards. Mr. Allen is frank about the difficulties he had in adjusting to retirement which, as he looks back upon it, could have been averted with proper preretirement counselling. (#361)

Although Mr. Allen says that the last ten years he spent with Manufacturing were the most satisfying of a long association, almost 40 years, he nevertheless elected to retire early, when he reached his 60th birthday. A major reason for retiring early was his feeling that he was becoming less and less content to work under supervision, particularly because of changes in supervisory personnel. But he also admits that his work no longer gave him the same satisfaction. All in all, he is very pleased with his retirement situation. His social life is more active and, he says, "I have great satisfaction in seeing our family business prosper with what seems to be a balanced leadership of all involved."

For one of our respondents who retired two years ago from Chain Store, a very satisfying 40-year career, at the end of which he was receiving about $50,000 a year as a marketing manager, proved to be the foundation for an even more satisfying full-time career with a manufacturing company, initially as a sales executive but now as executive vice-president and chief executive officer. Josh Green's plans for retirement were clear-cut. He knew several years in advance when he would leave Chain Store, and he had received an offer from his new employer before he retired. His salary is now somewhat higher than it was with Chain Store, but Mr. Green is satisfied with his present work for other reasons as well. His retirement was in part induced by his felief that he had risen as far as he could reasonably expect in Chain Store, and for that reason his job no longer provided the same challenge or satisfaction. He summarizes his postretirement experience in the following terms:

Having spent all my working years with one company and having had a very satisfying career with this great company, I felt I would like to try another career. I joined the Bingham Manufacturing Company, the fourth largest company of its kind and privately owned . . . Certainly without the administrative experience I had at Chain Store I could not operate in my present capacity. I find my present assignment satisfying and am enjoying these years as the fullest of my career. (#909)

The Path to Postretirement Work Experience

Although a quarter of our respondents had either thought about postretirement salaried employment or taken active steps with regard to it before they retired, only a very few (18) had actually received offers of postretirement salaried employment from other employers, offers which were instrumental in their decision to opt for early retirement. A much larger number, almost a third of the respondents, had either thought about or taken active steps with regard to postretirement consulting work or self-employment, even though again only a small number (50) actually reported that their decision to retire early was induced in part because of their belief that the time was opportune for them to engage in consulting work or self-employment, as was pointed out in Chapter 2.

Although only a few of the respondents retired because they had received attractive offers from other employers, those who actually worked as a salaried employee after retirement reported that they usually found employment without any real delay. About 70 of the respondents had already obtained salaried employment before they retired from their company. Of the other respondents who worked as salaried employees after retirement, two-thirds obtained a job within a month after they started looking. Only a handful said that they had to look for work longer than six months. Nevertheless, several respondents who had no postretirement work experience did tell us that they had made unsuccessful efforts to secure employment and that the lack of response to their efforts discouraged further attempts. The evidence does seem clear that most of those respondents who wanted to work as salaried employees after retirement were able to secure employment with a minimum of difficulty.

Not only did most respondents who wanted postretirement salaried employment find such work quickly, three out of five secured it through personal contacts. About one out of five obtained salaried employment in response to an advertisement, and about one in twelve received assistance from his company which led to a job. Only one respondent said that he had obtained postretirement salaried employment through an employment agency! The majority of respondents desiring postretirement salaried employment were able to utilize personal relationships developed before retirement as a springboard from which salaried employment could be quickly obtained.

Although they generally obtained jobs through personal contact and without undue delay, a conspicuous finding of our survey is that the postretirement salaried employment experience was usually quite different from preretirement employment experience. Prominent among these differences is the fact that the respondents usually worked for small- or medium-sized firms. More than half worked for firms that had less than 100 employees. Only one out of five worked for a firm employing 500 or more people.

Two-thirds of the respondents reported that their postretirement salaried job was quite different from what they had done before retirement. Only one out of ten said that their work was quite similar. Salaried employment after retirement, therefore, seems usually to have required an adjustment not only to a different organizational environment (i.e. a small firm in contrast to a giant national corporation), but also to quite different kinds of work. The adjustment, however, seems to have been made by the bulk of our respondents without great difficulty. One-third of the respondents said that they were more satisfied with their postretirement job than they had been with their preretirement job. More than a quarter said that their satisfaction with postretirement work was about the same as their satisfaction with preretirement work. Since the great majority of the respondents seem to have been quite satisfied with their preretirement work, a strong majority of the respondents seem to have looked upon their postretirement salaried work with a good deal of favor.

One-fifth of the respondents who had worked as salaried employees after retirement did indicate that they were less satisfied with their postretirement work experience than with their preretirement work. It is evident from the comments of some of these respondents that they were forced by economic pressure to accept jobs which they considered to be demeaning and poorly paid.

It will be recalled that almost two-thirds of our respondents had been managers before retirement. In striking contrast, three-quarters of the respondents who were employed at the time of the survey were engaged in professional or technical work. As one might expect, a higher proportion of the Manufacturer's respondents, over one-half, had been in professional or technical capacities before retirement. Eighty-five percent of the respondents from this company who were employed at the time of the survey were professionally or technically occupied. But even in the case of Chain Store, where more than three-quarters of the respondents had been managers prior to retirement, two-thirds of the respondents who were employed at the time of the survey termed their jobs professional or technical.

The moral is clear. Although it is possible for a manager to secure postretirement salaried employment relatively easily in most cases, and on occasion as a manager, it is more likely that he will have to adapt to a new role as a professional or technical employee, utilizing the skills that he had acquired as a manager to fulfill the new role.

Those of our respondents who had been managers before retirement were slightly less likely to be working at the time of the survey than were the respondents who had been employed as professionals or technicians. In addition, more than two-thirds of the preretirement managers who reported that they were working at the time of the survey said that their job was professional or technical in content. Those respondents whose preretirement experience was professional/technical in character and who were working at the time of the survey were overwhelmingly employed as professional/technical personnel. Only one out of eight reported that he was working as a manager, usually in a small firm.

The road to postretirement salaried work experience, in summary, requires considerable flexibility in work roles. Even if the road is relatively smooth for a good number of the retirees, there is little question that for some the pathway is difficult and tortuous, requiring painful adjustments to new tasks and lowered status. For others, the adjustment is so painful that postretirement salaried employment is soon given up. Some of the respondents who had moved to the sunbelt or to retirement communities indicated that a lack of job opportunities and the fact that those available were often of a menial character had precluded their working as salaried employees, even though in some cases they were eager to find such work.

On the other hand, the change in work environment and in work role was for some of our respondents a welcome part of their postretirement work experience, a relief from years of the same kind of work and a proving ground for new abilities and interests. It will be recalled that many of the respondents reported that their retirement decision was based in part upon their sense that they had reached a plateau and that their work no longer provided sufficient challenge and satisfaction. For many of these individuals, postretirement work experience has been a revitalizing experience because it offered new challenges and rich rewards, either economic or psychic or both.

For some of the respondents who had accepted relatively undemanding salaried employment, the very fact that their work was unpressured and their work schedule relatively flexible and relaxed was one of the major satisfactions of their postretirement work experience.

Postretirement salaried work experience differed greatly from preretirement work experience with respect to work schedules. As one would expect, preretirement work was almost always full time, full year. Although some of the respondents said that they would have appreciated an opportunity to "taper off" from full-time, full-year work schedules before their formal retirement commenced, the evidence is conclusive that few of them had such an option. A handful of the respondents retired after a period of illness during which they worked less than full time and full year.

One-half of the respondents reported that they had worked between 37 and 42 hours a week in the year before retirement. Slightly less than half reported that they had worked 43 hours per week or more: one-quarter of the respondents between 43 and 49 hours per week, and one-fifth of them 50 hours or more. Popular impressions that managers generally work 50 to 60 hours a week to the contrary, our respondents for the most part did not work excessively long hours.

Those respondents who said that they were working at the time of the survey generally were working part-time schedules. Even so, a third of them reported that they were working at least 37 hours a week, and one out of ten was working 43 hours or more per week. At the other extreme, one-quarter were working 12 hours or less per week, and another third were working between 13 and 24 hours a week.

When asked to indicate whether their postretirement salaried work experience was part time, full time, part year or full year, the respondents who had postretirement salaried work experience gave the following responses:

Work Schedule	Percent Distribution
Part time, part year	22
Full time, part year	15
Part time, full year	38
Full time, full year	25

When asked what work schedules they would have preferred, this same group of respondents with postretirement salaried work experience indicated that they would have preferred on balance slightly shorter and more flexible work schedules. The different between actual and preferred schedules was not a major problem for most of them and certainly not a source of major strain and discontent.

Nevertheless, one of the important advantages attributed to self-employment and consulting work after retirement by many respondents is the flexibility in hours that such work experience permits. Respondents who chose these forms of postretirement work experience were also much more likely to choose shorter work schedules. They were distributed between part time, full time, part year and full year work experience as follows:

Work Schedule	Percent Distribution
Part time, part year	43
Full time, part year	10
Part time, full year	34
Full time, full year	13

Respondents who chose to work after retirement or were forced by circumstances to work were made up of four groups: (1) salaried employees, (2) the self-employed, (3) consultants, and (4) those who combined two or more of the foregoing types of work experience. The salaried employee group was the largest of the four. Almost two out of five respondents with postretirement work experience elected salaried employment alone. The other three groups were about the same size, slightly more respondents electing consulting work than self-employment.

Since consulting work tended to be comparatively short in duration and intermittent compared to self-employment, at any one time more of the respondents were actually self-employed than engaged in consulting work. Aside from the consultant group, moreover, continuity of employment experience throughout the retirement period was characteristic of a majority of the respondents who had any work experience at all. Over 250 of the respondents (about a quarter) reported that they had either been working or looking for work during "most of the months since retirement." Since job search was generally quite short, usually less than a month in duration, the great majority of these respondents was actually working during most of their retirement. Associated with this continuity of work experience is the fact that more than two-thirds of the respondents who worked as salaried employees worked for only one employer during the period of their retirement.

For the great majority of the respondents who wanted to work after retirement or were forced to work, the decision to work was not an impulsive or temporary one. The high degree of continuity of work experience and continuity of employment with one employer is, we surmise, closely related to the fact that these same respondents had had, for the most part, decades of work experience with a single employer before retirement. But it may be of some significance to potential employers of retired managers and professional/technical personnel that most of those who want to work after retirement seem to be interested in stable and long-term employment opportunities, even if they also desire at the same moment somewhat shorter and more flexible work schedules.

Because of the relatively high degree of work continuity, the proportion of respondents who have had any work experience during retirement is not very different, though of course larger, than the proportion who were either at work or who worked at some time during the 12 months before the survey (see Table 3.1).

An examination of the proportions of respondents from the three companies who were working at the time of the survey or had worked during the previous 12 months throws light upon the importance of preretirement affiliation in relation to postretirement work status (see Table 3.2).

Whereas only one-fifth of the Utility respondents and one-fourth of the Manufacturer respondents were either at work at the time of the survey or had worked at some time in the previous 12 months, two-fifths of the Chain Store respondents were either working or had worked during the previous 12 months. Moreover, marked differences

Table 3.1 Distribution of Respondents' Work Experience during Retirement

	Percent Distribution of All Respondents	
Work Status	Worked at Some Time during Retirement	Working at Time of Survey or during Previous 12 Months
Salaried employee only	13	11
Self-employed only	8	8
Consultant only	9	6
Any combination of above	7	5
Subtotal	37	30
No work experience	63	70
Total	100%	100%

Table 3.2 Comparison of Respondents' Work Status by Employment before Retirement

Work Status	Percent Distribution by Present Work Status or Work during Past 12 Months		
	Manufacturing	Chain Store	Utility
Salaried employee only	7	17	9
Self-employed only	6	11	8
Consultant only	8	6	2
Combination	5	7	2
Subtotal	26	41	21
No work experience during past 12 months	74	59	79
Total	100%	100%	100%

in the kinds of work experience obtained by respondents from the three companies are evident. The great majority of the Chain Store and Utility respondents were engaged in salaried employment or self-employment. In contrast, the Manufacturer respondents were concentrated in consulting and self-employment.

The fact that such a high proportion of the Chain Store respondents were either working at the time of the survey or had worked during the previous 12 months is in large part explained by the economic pressures felt by this group. Rather than receiving a defined benefit pension, the Chain Store respondents had accumulated stock in Chain Store. Their postretirement income and asset position had been adversely affected by the behavior of the stock market. But it is also evident from this group of respondents that the decision to work after retirement is, for the majority of those who chose to work, only partly the result of economic pressures. We now turn to the complex of reasons for deciding to work after retirement and to the reasons for choosing particular types of work experience.

"I went back to work because. . . ."

Respondents who had performed any work for pay during their retirement were asked why they had gone back to work, either as salaried employees or as consultants and self-employed. They were given six possible choices:

1) I wanted more income for my spouse and myself (more income).
2) I wanted the income to help to contribute to the support of my children (child support).
3) I was very concerned about the effect of inflation upon my future standard of living (inflation).
4) I wanted more contact with people (contact with people).
5) Taken as a whole, I liked to keep working (liked working).
6) I was concerned that not working would have an adverse effect on my health (health).

On the average there were 2.3 responses per case, indicating that the decision to work during retirement was usually based upon a complex of reasons. Respondents could also check "other reasons" and specify these. About 20 percent of the respondents checked this box, but an examination of their remarks indicates that these were usually a specific variant of one of the six possibilities.

The most common reason for going back to work, given by three out of five respondents, was "liked working." This is of course consistent with the long tenure on the job and the numerous expressions of satisfaction with preretirement work experience volunteered by many respondents. It also helps to explain why the majority of the respondents who chose to work during retirement maintained this work status through most of their retirement.

The second most common reason for postretirement work experience, given by half of the respondents, was "more income." Related to income, particularly to future income, was the answer "inflation," given by two out of five of the respondents. Only a handful of respondents gave "child support" as a reason for postretirement work.

One-third of the respondents said that they had gone back to work because they wanted more contact with people, and one-quarter gave their concern that their health might suffer if they did not continue to work as one of their reasons for continuing to work.

Three of the reasons for continuing to work were noneconomic in character: "liked working," "contact with people" and "health." Somewhat to our initial surprise, but not surprising to us after we had had an opportunity to read the respondents' often lengthy descriptions of their postretirement work experience, these "noneconomic" reasons were given somewhat more frequently than the "economic" reasons. The decision to keep on working after retirement or to resume work after an interval of time was for the majority of those respondents who worked during retirement a complex process, in which those dimensions of work which are noneconomic in character played at least as important a part as the economic dimensions. In part this may be due to the fact that the overwhelming majority of our respondents could count upon relatively generous pensions and many had other sources of income and considerable accumulated assets. On the other hand, a number of the retirees had experienced substantial decreases in total family income upon retirement, and one group of them, the Chain Store respondents, had also been subjected to a major disappointment because of the effect of the behavior of the stock market on their retirement income and asset expectations.

The importance of noneconomic factors in the decision of many of our respondents to return to work or to continue to work during retirement is probably a reflection of the fact that they were managerial and professional/technical personnel whose work lives have for many decades been the source of important intrapersonal and interpersonal satisfactions. The comments of many of those who returned to work centered around their achievements and unusual qualifications. In the case of the relatively few who were retired involuntarily before mandatory retirement age, who were particularly apt to feel that the decision of their company to retire them reflected upon their achievements and their qualifications, the return to work, or continuation of work after retirement, often proved to themselves and the former superiors responsible for their retirement that the company's decision had been wrong and unjust.

By and large, the reasons given for returning to work or continuing to work during retirement by those who became salaried employees were much the same as those given by the self-employed and the consultants, but there are a few revealing differences in the patterns of responses. The self-employed were more likely to say that they had returned to work because they liked to work or were concerned that their health might suffer if they did not work. Consultants, on the other hand, were apt to emphasize the importance of contact with people. Consultants also gave considerably more specific and idiosyncratic reasons for returning to work: that it permitted travel, or was often associated with considerable status and a relatively high hourly or daily remuneration, or permitted them to continue quite specialized projects or technical and professional activities.

We anticipated that those respondents who chose either self-employment or consulting work after retirement might have done so because these two forms of continued work activity offered particularly attractive options after a lifetime of salaried employment. We also thought that in some cases a respondent might have chosen these forms of work activity because salaried employment was unobtainable. Respondents who were either self-employed or consultants at some time during their retirement were therefore asked to indicate why. Two out of five of these respondents said that they had always wanted to engage in these kinds of work activity. One out of five said that they could earn more income through consulting or self-employment than through salaried employment. But the most frequent reasons for choosing consulting and self-employment, mentioned by three out of five, were that these work activities would afford both more flexibility in work schedules and the opportunity to work as many more years as desired.

Only about one in ten chose consulting or self-employment because no salaried employment was available. It is clear that retirement afforded many respondents a long-sought opportunity to engage in consulting or self-employment and that these kinds of work activity were often felt as a liberation from rigid work schedules, conformity to organizational imperatives, and acceptance of unwelcome stress and conflict with superiors. It should be recalled, moreover, that a significantly larger proportion of respondents chose to be consultants or self-employed than chose to be salaried employees during retirement. And preference for consulting and self-employment was evident even in the planning stage of retirement.

Not to Work, That Is the Answer

A substantial minority of the respondents have worked at some time during their retirement, but a majority have not worked at all. The comments of those who have chosen not to work often bear eloquent testimony that they felt that they had worked long enough, that they were glad to turn over to their successors the responsibilities and headaches of managerial decisions, and that they found the nonwork activities offered by a financially comfortable retirement a more than satisfactory substitute for their preretirement work activities. Often they pointed out that their satisfaction with a retirement experience free of work was directly related to and based upon many years of highly satisfactory working life. For these individuals, the meaning of retirement seems clear. It offers an opportunity to do many things which have been postponed by many years of hard and demanding work. It means a comfortable change of pace and a sense of freedom. For many of these individuals, the refrain "retirement is wonderful" comes at the end of their comments.

A relatively small minority of those who have not worked, or are presently not working, wrote that they were deeply disappointed by the lack of opportunity to work. These were the individuals who were most likely to point to acts of discrimination against older workers; but in some cases they pointed out that health problems or, in the case of some who had relocated in retirement communities, the inevitable lack of job opportunities, were the primary reasons for their nonwork status.

Those respondents who were not presently at work or who had not worked in the past 12 months were asked to indicate why. One out of six indicated that they were not working because there was no opportunity in their own field. Only two percent said that the reason was lack of opportunity in any field. It is evident, therefore, that for those respondents who were not working because of a perception of a lack of job opportunities, most were highly selective about what jobs they considered appropriate. The barriers to postretirement work activity were for them largely associated with their belief that they could not continue to do work closely related to what they had done before retirement.

About one out of seven said that they were not working because of poor health. A far higher proportion, more than one-half of all those not working, indicated that they simply did not want to work any longer. But another major group of nonworkers said that they were not working because, after taxes and other deductions, there was insufficient incentive. Almost a third of those who were not working gave this as one of the explanations for their nonwork status. It should be noted that a minority of those who were not working gave more than one reason for their nonwork status.

Although a majority of those who were not working said that they did not want to work, a substantial proportion of nonworkers were interested in the possibility of working at some time in the future. For this group an improvement in job opportunities, a reduction of the tax disincentives, an increase in financial pressures, or some other change in circumstances might lead to a shift to some kind of work activity.

This group was asked what kind of work schedule they would prefer. Of the almost 300 respondents who fell into the category of those presently "not working but interested in employment," the overwhelming majority were interested in relatively short hours and, often, in flexible work schedules:

Preferred Work Schedule	Percent Distribution
Part time, part year	72
Full time, part year	8
Part time, full year	16
Full time, full year	4

A rough approximation of the total pool of workers, actual and potential, is provided by adding the total number of respondents who reported that they were at work to those who reported that they were interested in work but not presently at work. The two groups are approximately the same size, and taken together they constitute almost 60 percent of the respondents. It should be kept in mind, however, that the group of respondents who are presently not at work but interested in working contains a relatively large proportion of individuals who desire part-time, part-year work and flexible work schedules, and who place fairly strict limitations on the kind of work they are willing to perform and the remuneration needed to provide adequate incentives. For many of these respondents, the present Social Security earned income limitations and resulting heavy marginal tax rates are such serious disincentives that they will not consider work, even though they indicate that they would have no trouble finding well-paid consulting jobs.

The possibility that the Social Security disincentives will be sharply decreased and possibly even abolished in the next decade may mean a sizable increase in the number of managerial and professional/technical personnel who elect early retirement with the intention of exploiting improved opportunities to earn substantial amounts through part-time consulting work and self-employment.

Even with no reduction in the tax disincentives against post-retirement work, an increase in the rate of inflation and the consequent more rapid erosion of pension benefits and accumulated savings than had been anticipated may have a similar effect and may induce a substantial number of retirees not presently working to try to reenter the work arena. A number of respondents wrote that, although they were not presently working and did not want to work, they might not be able to afford the option of unemployed retirement much longer.

4

Unpaid Activities

After retirement, retirees shifted a great deal of their prior work time to various unpaid activities. Whereas before retirement most retirees had spent less than 20 hours per week in various unpaid pursuits such as volunteer work, hobbies, and domestic chores, in the past year, after retirement most retirees spent 30 hours a week or more in the same activities. Not surprisingly, the greater the number of hours spent working for pay after retirement, the fewer the number of hours allocated to unpaid activities.

Volunteer Work

One form of unpaid activity which corporate managers and professional/technical workers commonly engage in both before and after retirement is volunteer work. A male Manufacturing retiree presently not working for pay, who retired in 1970 at the age of 61 after 28 years in sales and marketing with a current family income of $15,000, wrote:

I suggest that a meaningful, challenging and enjoyable retirement entails the substitution of a self-ordered scheduling of events, to replace the highly ordered business life prior to retirement.

My initial tendency was to jump into too many commitments—I have now backed off somewhat and feel quite comfortable.

Volunteer activities represent the most satisfying aspect of my retirement. [He now spends 15-20 hours per week in volunteer work.]

I am president of a church-sponsored nonprofit corporation, building housing for limited-income elderly in our community.

I joined the local chapter of SCORE and get much satisfaction from this volunteer counseling of small businesses in the community. (#105)

Another respondent, a male Manufacturing retiree presently not working for pay, who retired in 1972 at the age of 62 after 25 years in sales, personnel and engineering with a current family income of less than $7,000, wrote:

I have and enjoy a natural ability to teach elementary school children (grades 1-6) *under the direction* of a good (college-trained elementary school) teacher. Rewards are a better understanding of such things as patience, tolerance, fortitude, etc., within one's self and a greater love and respect for those with (*and without*) learning disabilities.

Spouse has learned to use a camera *well* and creates slide programs for an elementary school library—which are welcomed with pleasure by both principal and teachers. 'Kids' enjoy them too. (#326)

This retiree also spends more than 16 hours per week in volunteer work.

One retiree felt very strongly that volunteer work is an obligation of the retired. He is a male Manufacturing retiree who retired six years ago at the age of 62 after 42 years in production. Currently not working for pay, he volunteers one hour per week and has a current family income of $19,000. He writes:

The talent and experience of a retiree should be given away as 'bread cast upon the waters' and not for 'pieces of silver.' (#262)

Fifty-four percent of our sample were involved in volunteer work before retirement and 57 percent in the past year. The number of hours spent volunteering after retirement increased slightly, but not substantially. Females devoted more hours to volunteer work than male retirees, as they did to other unpaid activities (with the exception of home maintenance). Most volunteers spent one to five hours per week in volunteer work both before and after retirement. Those volunteers spending six to ten hours per week increased from 17% to 25% of volunteers, and those spending longer periods of time also increased slightly. Most volunteers were satisfied with the amount of hours they allocated to it, although over one-third of present volunteers indicated that they would prefer to spend more time per week in volunteer activities. Factors which may inhibit increased participation may be lack of access to effective volunteer-based organizations, a feeling that volunteer work is not a sufficient replacement for work and does not make adequate use of resources and talents, and/or a feeling that the volunteer activities available are not sufficiently fulfilling. Age, on the other hand, did not influence volunteerism. A male Manufacturing retiree with a current family income of $13,000, who retired five years ago at the age of 62 after 43 years in engineering and does not work for pay but does devote 15 hours per week to volunteer work, complained:

Our intent, during the years in our retirement was to give freely of our time and energy for service to others. We presently realize only a fragment of our expectations from such involvement.

In general, society to date fails to plan for, to organize, to implement goals and objectives which will motivate and involve the so-called elderly senior citizens to help those who lack the ability to help themselves. (#203)

The better educated, who are most likely to feel this way, are still more likely to volunteer than those with less formal education.

Current family income also played a role in the decision to volunteer. Those with higher total family incomes were more likely to be volunteers after retirement, but not necessarily to devote more time to volunteer activities, than those with lower total family incomes.

Almost half of volunteers worked for religious organizations, about one-fifth for political organizations. A lesser degree of participation was found in health, social and business organizations utilizing volunteer labor. Those with a smaller total family income and less educational background were more attracted to volunteer work in religious organizations, whereas other types of organizations were more attractive to the more affluent and better educated.

Whether a retiree was a volunteer or not affected the degree of satisfaction with retirement. Those who had done volunteer work within the past year were more likely to be highly satisfied, although the number of hours per week spent as a volunteer was not related to satisfaction. Neither was satisfaction related to the extent to which their volunteer activities resembled their preretirement career activities.

Hobbies and Recreation

Other unpaid activities which received increased participation after retirement were hobbies and recreation. A typical example is a 64-year-old Chain Store retiree who retired in 1974 after 26 years in sales and marketing with a present family income of $17,000. Currently not working for pay, he spends 8 hours a week at his hobbies and recreation. He describes his activities:

The first thing I did when I retired was to build a wood shop. My wife and I spent time looking for antiques. We are putting them in our home now—some day I may sell some. I have just spent a year and a half building and carving a curved glass china cabinet. (#966)

A 74-year-old male Manufacturing retiree, who retired in 1969 after 43 years in research and development who currently has a family income of $16,000 and is not working for pay, devotes 50 hours a week to his hobbies and recreational activities. He wrote:

The first year after my retirement we took a 15,000-mile trip around the U.S. in our travel trailer. After that we started spending our winters in the Southwest in a large travel-trailer court where there was adequate opportunity to enjoy our hobbies and do volunteer work in connection with them.

After pulling our travel trailer back and forth between Arizona and New York for four years, we traded it in on a park model, which we have here the year around, and just drive the car each way.

My principal hobbies are rock cutting and polishing, silver-smithing and photography. (#347)

Before retirement, 38 percent of the persons in our sample spent between one and five hours per week on their hobbies and on recreation. Another 33 percent spent between six and 10 hours per week. Ten percent claimed to have no hobbies or recreation. After retirement, the percentage of people spending 11 hours or more per week on hobbies and recreation increased from 19 percent to 59 percent. Eight percent still claimed to spend no time at hobbies and recreation. People who had no hobbies nor much recreational activity before retirement were not apt to develop these interests afterwards.

Hobbies and recreation and volunteer work operated somewhat as replacements for each other in how one chose to spend one's time. A greater number of hours spent at hobbies and recreation was generally associated with fewer or no hours spent volunteering.

In the area of satisfaction, hobbies and recreational pursuits were also interchangeable with volunteering. In general, those who had hobbies or were involved in recreational activities were more likely to be very satisfied with their retirement. Unlike volunteering, there was a direct relationship between the number of hours spent in hobbies and recreation and the degree of satisfaction with retirement. Sometimes, retirement freed retirees to transform a hobby into a major focus of their lives, perhaps even to change a hobby to a remunerative activity, which also contributed to increased satisfaction. For example, a 65-year-old male Manufacturing retiree, who retired five years ago to devote the rest of his life to art after 31 years in all aspects of technical work for his company, had a current family income of $11,000, partially due to income from his artwork. He wrote:

With the possible exception of my experience in World War II, I am working longer and harder than at any time in my life. Retirement has afforded me the opportunity to accomplish the goals for which I feel I was destined, and hopefully, within the next year I should be reaping the rewards of my endeavors. I feel like a young man with his future ahead of him, in spite of the fact that I had a severe coronary in '62 and 32 cobalt treatments for a throat operation in '67. I am striving for acknowledgment as an aviation and Western artist.

Without my investments, my pension and Social Security, I would not have had the time and the wherewithal to accomplish this. (#767)

Table 4.1 shows the general pattern of frequency of the respondents' engagement in various hobbies and forms of recreation, both in the year before retirement and in the past 12 months. Although there are increases in the numbers engaging "frequently" in all of the activities listed in Table 4.1, with the exception of technical and business-related reading, the biggest increases tend to be in the areas of active sports, general household repair, gardening and travel (which will be discussed separately).

Table 4.1 Frequency of Hobbies and Recreational Activities before Retirement and in Past 12 Months[a] (in percent)

	Never			Frequently		
	(1) Before	(2) Past 12 Months	Change (2 minus 1)	(3) Before	(4) Past 12 Months	Change (4 minus 3)
Reading newspaper	2	2	0	77	89	+12
TV	8	5	− 3	38	52	+14
Gardening	36	25	−11	28	47	+19
General household repair	18	14	− 4	14	46	+32
Active sports	42	32	−10	16	39	+23
Travel	19	13	− 6	13	37	+24
Technical business reading	21	37	+16	50	30	−20
Reading current fiction	57	47	−10	12	22	+10
Reading general nonfiction	45	38	− 7	14	21	+ 7
Card games	55	51	− 4	9	16	+ 7
Woodworking	68	62	− 6	7	16	+ 9
Other arts and crafts	79	72	− 7	5	12	+ 7
Theater	47	42	− 5	6	10	+ 4
Photography	65	62	− 3	6	9	+ 3
Music	82	79	− 3	4	8	+ 4
Sports events	59	58	− 1	4	6	+ 2
Adult education	74	73	− 1	5	6	+ 1
Reading literary classics	78	71	− 7	3	5	+ 2
Painting	95	92	− 3	2	3	+ 1

[a]Based on number of valid cases; this varies from 1031 to 1037.

Males are slightly more likely to engage frequently in active sports. Those involved in participant sports are also likely to be younger, more satisfied with retirement, and more likely to report improvement in both their health and social life since retirement. A male Manufacturing retiree, who retired in 1970 at the age of 60 after 42 years in research and development who is currently not working for pay, with a family income of $25,000, spends approximately 10 hours per week at physical fitness:

I believe the human body should be maintained and used both

mentally and physically because *"what you don't use, you lose."*

There is a nice YMCA within one block of our house. On retiring I joined up and started swimming for 30 minutes daily at 11:30 a.m. There I preceded it by jogging one mile on the one-eighth-mile track every day. This is now two miles per day. I have also joined a physical fitness class at 6:00 p.m. on three evenings per week for one hour of exercises and more jogging. This totals to approximately 10 hours per week at the YMCA. I started the program in 1970—my weight was 170 lbs.—resting heart beat 74 beats per minute—blood pressure 162/98. Most recent test results: weight 150 lbs.—resting heart beat 61—blood pressure 120/80. In addition, I spend time daily sawing and chopping wood for our fireplace to help heat our home. I eat three square meals and rest after meals, catching up on reading newspapers and *Wall St. Journal* as well as weekly magazines. My wife and I go shopping frequently and I give her a hand washing the dishes and running the vacuum cleaners. Evenings after supper we watch some TV and catch up on reading. Gardening is a major item starting late May thru October. Some travel during April and Nov. to visit our two sons, 31 and 35 years old at Travis AFB Cal. and Fitzsimmons Army Medical Center, Denver, Colo. by plane to appease my wife (5 grandchildren). (#055)

Those who attend sports events are also more likely to be younger, whereas older retirees tend to engage in general household repair, arts and crafts, newspaper, magazine and general nonfiction reading, and adult education classes.

Whereas males are more likely to engage in general household repair, woodworking, photography, watching television, reading technical and business related materials, and active and spectator sports, females are more likely to paint, do arts and crafts, attend the theater, be involved in music, read current fiction, newspapers, magazines and general nonfiction, and attend adult education classes. There were no sex differences in participation in gardening.

Educational differences were also present among those who chose various postretirement activities. Those with more formal education were more attracted to the theater, watching television, photography, the reading of literary classics, general nonfiction and technical and business-related matter, and adult education courses, whereas lesser-educated retirees are more likely to engage in woodworking, and the reading of newspapers and magazines.

Higher preretirement salaries also predisposed retirees to different interests and activities after retirement: theater attendance, painting, photography, and the reading of most types of materials. In general, activities likely to be of interest before retirement remained of interest or became increasingly attractive after retirement.

Routine Domestic Chores and Home Maintenance

Not working for pay also freed retirees to spend more time working on their homes, although many retirees did not exercise this option to any great extent. One retiree with a present family income of $22,000, a male Manufacturing employee who retired in 1976 at the age of 62 after 39 years in research and development, even returned to work (consulting) after retirement to avoid having to do household chores:

My biggest problem after retirement was being available around
the house for trivial chores I didn't want to do. The work I am
doing now provides an escape from this. (#119)

Most retirees spent one to five hours per week at routine domestic chores in the year before their retirement. After retirement, a substantial number (32 percent) still spent only one to five hours at this activity, but the number of those spending more than ten hours also increased. Trends in the allocation of time to home maintenance were very similar.

Unlike volunteer work and hobbies and recreation, those who did spend more time at either routine domestic chores or home maintenance were less-satisfied with their retirement. This illustrates the importance of self-enriching activities to the retiree, more than merely filling one's spare time with "busy work."

Variations in Time Allocation: Travel and
Seasonal Recreation

Although most retirees reported that the time per week they allocated to the above activities was fairly consistent, varying only moderately to little or not at all, those who did report variation generally attributed it to the disruption of their routine by travel or seasonal recreation. Thirty-two percent reported that their allocated time varied due to seasonal recreation, and 27 percent reported that travel altered their general arrangements.

A male Manufacturing retiree presently not working for pay, who retired two years ago at the age of 60 after 28 years in research, development and production with a present family income of $10,000, wrote, for example:

My wife and I had spent 12 to 18 hours working and building on the side, so we had never had much time for anything else. So we sold the house in town. We live at the lake in the summer and go to Florida winters. This year we spent six months in Europe; now I will have a restful summer at the lake.

I had bronchial asthma while I worked; after about three months in Florida it disappeared. (#388)

Another retiree, from Chain Store, presently not working for pay, retired 10 years ago at the age of 55 after 34 years in sales and marketing with a current family income of $15,000. He wrote:

My wife and I also found that having a second home in Mexico, where we spend four to six months each year, has been a great alternative for us. This had kept us interested and active through the years. (#446)

A few retirees had altered their time-use pattern so that travel and/or seasonal recreation occupied the bulk of their time throughout the year.

A Manufacturing retiree, who retired at 60 years of age in 1972 after 42 years in accounting with a present family income of $19,000, reported:

My wife and I have completely changed our lifestyle since retirement. For the first couple of years we traveled around the country to see sights and country (historical and scenic) I wanted to see. Then we joined the Wally Byam Caravan Club International and have greatly enjoyed new friends and a new lifestyle. We live in a 31-foot AIRSTREAM trailer—spend seven months in winter in a park in Melbourne, Fla., where we have every kind of activity. We dance and square dance and party all winter. Then in summer we travel about—stop and spend some days with children and grandchildren and rest of time traveling to rallies in caravans and sightseeing from Canada through 48 states and Mexico.

My goal in trying to retire early was to be able to do just this kind of thing before either my wife, who is older, or I become ill or unable to physically do as we have been doing for six years now. (#629)

Another retiree, from Utility, retired in 1968 at the age of 61 after 45 years in equipment manufacturing with a current family income of $16,000. He wrote:

We planned on traveling. Since retirement we sold our home and moved into an apartment for one year. We then put our things in storage and moved into our travel trailer for seven and a half years. During this time we toured 17 European countries, Canada (east to west, including Newfoundland and Prince Edward Island), Mexico, and all of the Central American countries to the Panama Canal and end of Pan American Highway. After another year in an apartment we are back in our trailer, full time again.

As long as our health continues we plan on being on the road or on a travel trailer lot we own in Florida. (#971)

Overall, the number of those who said they traveled frequently increased from 13 percent before retirement to 37 percent after retirement. Retirees who had done some traveling prior to retirement tended to increase the extent to which they engaged in this activity. The percentage of those who had never traveled decreased only from 19 percent before retirement to 13 percent after retirement.

Traveling after retirement was also very much related to satisfaction with retirement and to a sense of improved health and an improved social life since retirement. Not surprisingly, those with a higher present family income were more able to take advantage of the increased opportunity to travel.

Withdrawal from Activity

A small number (9 percent) of retirees manifested a very low pattern of involvement in both paid work and unpaid activities after retirement. One retiree, who has not withdrawn from activity himself, commented on the lack of activity of other retirees in his community:

Since we are now living in a retirement community, I have many opportunities to view retirees in action. Most are a very resilient and adaptive people. However, many are far from happy, adjusted or psychologically well off. This is especially true of a group characterized as follows:

1. The widowed (male or female) who are not meeting or have not met their needs for reidentifying self in their single role.

2.   Those with an ill mate whose health condition means semiconfinement for the spouse.
3.   Those advanced enough in years so as to limit their activities and mobility. Many of these have lost all their peers due to death and, at the same time, their families are far removed from the scene.

The above respondent retired from Utility in 1975 at the age of 55 after 38 years in systems planning. He currently has a family income of $20,000, a significant part of which comes from his teaching of developmental psychology and marriage and family counseling. He goes on to observe that many of the retirees with whom he comes in contact, although financially secure, are withdrawn and de-pressed and live basically empty lives. He criticizes the lack of programs and program coordination in community, church and civic groups and calls for the recruitment of trained personnel to work with the retired to help restore their dignity and sense of purpose.

Those with a low pattern of involvement in both paid and unpaid activities typically tend to be male and to have less education than the other retirees in our sample. They are also more likely to be older— particularly 68 years and over—and to feel that their health has become worse since retirement (21 percent of low-activity retirees reported this, compared to 8 percent of the rest of the retirees). Low-activity retirees are also more likely to be involuntarily retired and tend to earn less money. Their preretirement salary is generally under $24,000, the low-income end of our sample, and their present total family income tends to be under $20,000. This group is also generally more surprised by their retirement experiences, having had a different set of expectations, perhaps one of these being the expectation of a higher degree of activity than the pattern they actually found themselves in.

The following two case examples perhaps best summarize the usual range of options in involvement in unpaid activities after retirement.

Cary McGovern is an example of very low involvement in unpaid activities throughout most of the year. He has done no volunteer work in the past 12 months and spends only four hours per week on hobbies and recreation. During the summer, however, he spends most of his time at a summer cottage on the shore. There he spends approximate-ly four hours a week at routine domestic chores and home mainte-nance and improvement, but during most of the year he spends 32 hours per week at salaried employment, feeling that he "couldn't sit around doing nothing after a few months of retirement" (#824). His frequent unpaid activities include card games, television, music, arts and crafts, and the reading of newspapers and magazines; but he has developed no new activity interests, nor has he increased the time spent at any of his previous interests, other than the summer cottage. He is a high school graduate who worked 39 years in production for the Utility before retiring in 1976 at the age of 57. His current income is $15,000, and he is very satisfied with his retirement.

Mr. Morton, on the other hand, does not work for pay at all but spends over 30 hours a week volunteering for an agency in the health and social welfare field. He spends only about a half-hour a week, however, at hobbies and recreation and spends little time working on his home. His family income is substantially higher than Mr. McGovern's ($50,000 per year), and he is extremely satisfied with the volunteer work his income has freed him to engage in:

Aside from the variety of things I do, aside from the fact that I can awaken every morning knowing I *have* things to do, I find my horizons have broadened immeasurably and my (our) friendships have expanded beyond any and all expectations. (#238)

Other unpaid activities in which he is interested are card games, television, and the reading of newspapers, magazines and current fiction. Mr. Morton is a college graduate who worked 38 years in research and development for Chain Store before retiring in 1972 at the age of 62.

5

Varieties of Postretirement Experiences: Major Subgroups

In this chapter we turn to the comparative postretirement experiences of major subgroups of our respondents. The dimensions along which these subgroups are arranged include the following: (1) date of retirement—slightly less than half of the respondents retired between 1968 and 1972, the rest between 1973 and 1977; (2) age at retirement—slightly less than half the respondents were under age 62 when they retired, the balance (with very few exceptions) were between 62 and 65; (3) age at the time of the survey—about two-fifths of the respondents were 65 or less at the time of the survey, about a third between 66 and 69, and just under 30 percent were 70 or over. It is on the basis of these three characteristics—date of retirement, age at retirement and present age—that we will initially contrast retirement experience. Later in the chapter we will turn to other characteristics, particularly sex.

Date of Retirement

A major objective of the Retirement Activities Study was to contrast the behavior of middle-level managerial and professional/technical personnel who had retired relatively recently with those who had retired somewhat earlier. For this purpose we have divided the ten-year period 1968-1977, during which almost all of our respondents retired, into four subgroups: (1) 1968-1969, (2) 1970-1972, (3) 1974-1975, and (4) 1976-1977. Each of these subgroups is called in subsequent pages a "vintage." For example, those respondents who retired in 1968 or 1969 are said to have been in Vintage 1, those in 1976-1977, Vintage 4.

Our panel was drawn so that each of the ten years between 1968 and 1977 would have been equally represented if every individual chosen had actually responded. In actual fact, the distribution of respondents came fairly close to this distribution:

Year of Retirement	Percent Share of Respondents
1968 — 1969, Vintage 1	17
1970 — 1972, Vintage 2	29
1973 — 1975, Vintage 3	32
1976 — 1977, Vintage 4	22

Recent years were slightly overrepresented, probably because respondents in relatively poor health tended to respond, we believe, somewhat less frequently than did those in relatively good health. Many individuals who retired in 1968-1969 would have been in their middle seventies at the time of the survey, and almost certainly more members of this vintage had severe health problems than did the members of the more recent vintages.

Since many of our questions dealt with the retirement decision itself and what leads up to it, including the planning process, some of our respondents were asked to think about and recall circumstances, opinions, attitudes and feelings which took place a number of years earlier. A certain degree of caution is therefore in order when iterpreting the answers of these early vintages, particularly when opinions and feelings are being examined. On the other hand, we have been impressed with the consistency of the answers of the respondents and the care with which they answered questions designed to probe such areas. Moreover, the differences in the behavior and attitudes of those respondents who retired, for example in 1968-1969, when compared with recent retirees seem to make a good deal of sense.

First of all, how do the four vintages evaluate their retirement experience. Was it what they expected and has the experience been satisfactory? Two questions in the survey address these issues. We have already called attention to the fact that most of the respondents reported that their expectations were more or less borne out and that their retirement experience has been at least moderately satisfactory.

With the exception of the subgroup that retired between 1973 and 1975, there is little difference between the four vintages with respect to how well expectations about retirement were met. And even in the case of Vintage 3, the difference largely turns on whether expectations have been very much met or fairly well met. Since members of the earlier vintages have had a longer time in which to have experienced unexpected turns of events, the high proportion of respondents in the early vintages who report that retirement experiences have been either very much similar or fairly similar to what they had expected is impressive. Moreover, in all four vintages only a very small percentage of respondents, never more than four percent, reported that retirement has been not at all what they expected. It is possible that some of those who did not respond to the questionnaire may have had retirement experiences which were quite different from what they had expected (e.g. health much worse than they had anticipated), and the nonrespondents may also have included a high proportion of those who were most disappointed and dissatisfied with their retirement experiences; but even with these caveats, the conclusion seems obvious. Both the earlier and the more recent vintages of retirees had retirement experiences which more or less met their expectations.

All vintages displayed much the same pattern of satisfaction with their retirement experience, although Vintage 3 was somewhat less frequently "very satisfied" than the other three vintages, but no more apt to be dissatisfied. The fact that the early vintages have a somewhat higher proportion of respondents reporting that they are "very satisfied" with retirement as a whole indicates that retirement satisfaction tends to be long-lived, not at all a product of a temporary euphoria caused by no longer having to meet hectic work schedules and the pressures of demanding jobs. In fact, it might be hazarded that the explanation for the slightly lower proportion of the more recent vintages who report great satisfaction with retirement may be that some individuals in these vintages were still in the process of adjusting to the absence of the satisfactions and stimulations of work when they answered the questionnaire.

Against the pattern, common to all vintages, of a generally high level of satisfaction with retirement and a feeling that expectations about retirement have been more or less met, how have the members of the four vintages used the hours made available by retirement from their companies? We have distinguished three major areas of time-use: (1) work experience as salaried employee, as consultant, or in self-employment, or some combination of the three; (2) voluntary service; and (3) a wide range of other activities: domestic chores, household maintenance, hobbies and recreation. Some differences (and more commonalties) emerge when the experiences with respect to these uses of time by members of the four vintages are compared.

First, the amount of and kind of work experience during retirement is only moderately affected by the year of retirement. The vintage that retired in 1968-1969 had the lowest rate of work experience, but even in their case about three out of ten respondents have engaged in some kind of work for pay during retirement. The two vintages 1970-1972 and 1973-1975 had the highest rate of work experience, about four out of ten. For the vintage 1976-1977, there was a slight fall-off in rate of work experience, but it should be borne in mind that the rate of work experience during retirement is a cumulative rate.

Some individuals who retired in 1976-1977 and did not choose to work during the first or second year of retirement will eventually engage in some kind of paid work, so it is likely that the rate of work experience for these recent retirees will eventually equal or exceed that of retirees from the earlier time periods. As it is, more than a third of the retirees who had retired during 1976 and 1977 had worked at some time during their retirement. With continued high rates of inflation, it is likely that a significant proportion of retirees of the vintage 1976-1977 who had not yet done any work, either as a salaried employee, consultant or self-employed individual, will reconsider their nonwork status.

Respondents were asked why they had sought postretirement paid employment, either as salaried employees or in the form of consulting work or self-employment. Significant differences are evident in the answers given by the most recent vintage compared with the oldest vintage. Members of the oldest vintage were much less likely to point to economic pressures, such as a need for more current income or concern about inflation. Only about a quarter mention need for income, and only one out of seven reported that concern about inflation had led to their decision to seek salaried employment. In sharp contrast, one out of two respondents from the most recent vintage who were working as salaried employees at the time of the survey reported that one of the reasons for their decision to seek salaried employment was the need for additional income, and one out of three mentioned a concern about inflation. While three out of four of the oldest vintage said that they had engaged in salaried employment after retirement because they liked to work, only one out of four of the most recent vintage gave their liking for work as a reason for seeking salaried employment.

The same differences emerge in the reasons given for seeking consulting work but, interestingly, one of the reasons mentioned more frequently by the recent vintage for engaging in consulting work rather than salaried employment is that consulting work may permit them to work more years than salaried employment would. It will be recalled that the most recent vintage was much more likely to choose consulting work than was the oldest vintage.

Retirees from the vintages 1970–1972 and 1973–1974 not only had the highest rates of postretirement work experience, but they were more apt to be salaried employees than were retirees from the other two vintages, 1968–1969 and 1976–1977. Of particular interest (and perhaps a straw in the wind) is the fact that retirees from the most recent vintage, 1976–1977, were more likely to choose self-employment or consulting work than were the two earlier vintages. The oldest vintage, 1968–1969, also had a relatively small proportion of salaried employees.

In general terms, then, a comparison of the postretirement work experience of the four vintages may demonstrate a tendency toward higher rates of postretirement work experience for the most recent retirees and possibly a trend toward consulting and self-employment in place of salaried employment as the favored postretirement work experience.

Continuity of work experience during the retirement period is another significant aspect of postretirement activity. While the oldest vintage, 1968–1969, has a lower rate of work experience, individuals in this vintage who chose to work displayed a high degree of continuity of work experience. In the case of this vintage, continuity of work experience means that a person was either working or looking for work during most of the months of his or her retirement, a period lasting some nine or ten years after retirement (it will be recalled that the length of the job search was usually quite short).

While about three out of ten respondents in the oldest vintage had some work experience, two out of ten said that this work experience was more or less continuous. Moreover, at the time they responded to the questionnaire, nine out of ten were at least 68 years old and one-half were 72 or over! Those individuals who retired in 1967–1968 and thereafter chose to work are usually strongly attached to the labor force; this attachment, for a large majority, has lasted through most of their retirement.

There were several respects in which the work experience of the four vintages differed, and other respects in which their experiences were quite similar. The early vintages, 1968-1969 and 1970-1972, were more apt to find salaried employment either in firms with less than 100 employees or in firms with at least 500 employees. Recent retirees, on the other hand, tended to avoid firms with 500 or more employees.

Three out of four of the respondents in the oldest vintages who had salaried work experience said that their postretirement salaried jobs were quite different from their preretirement work, whereas only one out of two retirees in the most recent vintage felt that his salaried work was quite different. Very few, only about one in ten in any of the vintages, felt that their postretirement salaried work was very similar in content to their preretirement job.

Broadly speaking, those respondents from the four vintages who were salaried employees tended to work the same kind of schedules, with one prominent exception. A larger proportion of the oldest vintage who were salaried employees said that they were working full time full year, almost two out of five compared with less than one out of five in the most recent vintage. Moreover, a larger proportion of these same individuals indicated that they preferred full-year full-time work schedules. Indeed, those members of the oldest vintage who were salaried employees overwhelmingly indicated that they wanted full-year work schedules. Three out of four favored full-year work and three out of ten preferred full-time work for the entire year! In contrast, in the case of the most recent vintage, those individuals who were salaried employees at the time of the survey overwhelmingly preferred part-time work, some four out of five. Three out of five indicated that their preference was for part-time work for the entire year. The most recent vintage indicated that, even where they were willing to be salaried employees, they much preferred shorter hours than their preretirement work schedules had permitted them to enjoy. The relatively frequent comment of our respondents that they might have considered delaying retirement if it had been possible to "taper off" in the length and intensity of work is confirmed by the kind of work schedules they say they would now prefer.

While the proportion of respondents who have had some kind of work experience in retirement is highest for the two intermediate vintages of 1970-1972 and 1973-1975, a different pattern emerges when a comparison is made of the present work status of respondents by vintage. (It will be recalled that we have defined present work status to mean working for pay at the time of the survey or at any time during the previous 12 months, in order not to exclude those individuals who work part-year schedules or intermittently.) There is a clear-cut pattern of higher rates of present work status for the more recent vintages. The differences between the oldest and the most recent vintages are indeed quite large, as Table 5.1 reveals:

Table 5.1 Present Work Status of the Four Vintages of Retirees (in percent)

Vintage	Total	Not Employed	Salary Only	Self-employment Only	Consultant Only	Any Combination
1968—1969	100	81	5	7	4	4
1970—1972	100	73	10	6	5	6
1973—1975	100	68	15	8	6	4
1976—1977	100	65	10	12	9	5

While only one out of five of the respondents in the oldest vintage reported that they were either presently engaged in paid work or had engaged in such activity during the previous 12 months, one out of three of the most recent vintage had some kind of paid work experience either at present or in the previous 12 months. Salaried employment for the oldest vintage was uncommon, only one out of twenty respondents having such work status. At the opposite extreme, one out of four of the most recent vintage were engaged either in self-employment or consulting work, or some combination of work status involving consulting or self-employment.

Respondents were asked how they had obtained their present or most recent salaried employment and how long they had searched for it. As might be expected, a higher proportion (two out of three) of the most recent vintage of retirees, those retiring in 1976–1977, reported that they had obtained their present or most recent job through personal contacts; but even in the case of the oldest vintage, retired in 1968–1969, one out of two reported that they had obtained their present or most recent salaried employment through personal contacts. More surprising is that almost one out of five of the oldest vintage reported that they had obtained their present or most recent salaried employment through the assistance of the company from which they had retired, whereas almost none of the most recent vintage reported such assistance.

When asked how long they had searched for their present or most salaried employment, two out of five of the respondents from the oldest vintage reported that they had obtained their present or most recent salaried employment before they retired from their company. Only one out of four respondents in the most recent vintage, 1976–1977, reported that they obtained their present or most recent salaried employment before they retired. On the other hand, a much higher proportion, one out of four, of the oldest vintage also reported that they had looked for more than six months for their present or most recent salaried employment. Practically none of the members of the most recent vintages, 1973–1975 and 1976–1977, reported that they had searched as long as six months for their present or most recent salaried employment.

Members of the oldest vintage also seem to have been somewhat more satisfied with their present or most recent salaried employment than were members of the other vintages. We have noted, however, that members of the recent vintages were more likely to have engaged in self-employment or consulting work than were members of the earlier vintages. While less satisfied with salaried employment than were the older vintages, the most recent vintages were much more satisfied with both consulting work and self-employment. This is particularly the case with the most recent vintage. When asked to compare the satisfactions from their consulting work or self-employment with the satisfactions of their preretirement job, two out of three respondents from the most recent vintage indicated that their consulting work or self-employment was more satisfying. Only one out of six indicated that they were less satisfied. The same pattern of satisfaction is evident in the case of the vintage 1973–1975.

NONWORK ACTIVITIES

An examination of patterns of time use in voluntary service reveals little difference among the four vintages, with the exception of slight fall-off in time devoted to voluntary service in the case of the most recent vintage. This is probably related to the fact that members of the most recent vintage were less engaged in volunteer work before retirement than were members of the other vintages.

Indeed, it is the consistency of the patterns of time use among the four vintages which is most striking when a detailed examination is made of hours spent in the major categories we have identified:

volunteer service, hobbies and recreation, domestic chores, and home maintenance. In spite of the years which separate the most recent vintages from the oldest vintages and the greater age of the latter, particularly those who retired in 1968-1969 when compared to those who retired in 1976-1977, there is no evidence of any major trend to fewer hours devoted per week to any of these major activity areas, with the exception of home maintenance where higher proportions of the two most recent vintages spend large amounts of time in home maintenance.

There is at most only a small difference between the most recent and the oldest vintages in patterns of time use and intensity of time use in major activities. This would seem to indicate that for retired middle-level managers and professional/technical personnel, there may now exist fairly clear-cut norms about time-use patterns which cut across age differences and differences in the length of retirement, at least within the age span and the differences in length of retirement dealt with by the Retirement Activities Study.

We do not want to imply that these norms apply to all members of an age group or vintage. Quite the contrary. Another important aspect of the patterns of time use is their variability for a given vintage. For example, members of the oldest and the most recent vintages reported the following hours spent per week in volunteer work and home maintenance in the past 12 months:

Table 5.2 Hours Spent per Week in Volunteer Work and Home Maintenance

Vintage	Number of Hours per Week: percent distribution				
	None	1—6	7—12	13 or More	Total Percent
Volunteer					
1968—1969	38	38	15	9	100
1976—1977	46	33	12	8	100
Home maintenance					
1968—1969	13	42	24	20	100
1976—1977	14	34	24	29	100

Perhaps of even greater significance is the distribution of hours spent in the major nonpaid work categories we have distinguished: (1) volunteer work (2) domestic chores (3) hobbies and recreation, and (4) home maintenance, when summed together.

Table 5.3   Number of Hours Spent per Week in All Nonpaid Work Activities
             (percent distribution)

	1−10	11−20	21−30	31−40	41−60	More than 60
1968−1969	21	45	17	9	7	2
1970−1972	23	40	18	13	4	2
1973−1975	19	42	22	10	5	3
1976−1977	21	40	18	14	6	1

While there is little difference between the distribution of hours of time spent in all nonpaid work activities by vintage, the distribution of hours worked per week for pay by vintage does differ considerably between the oldest and the more recent vintages as Table 5.4 indicates.

Table 5.4   Total Hours Worked For Pay per Week (percent distribution)

	None	1−20	21−40	41−50	More than 50
1968−1969	79	14	2	4	0
1970−1972	72	21	3	3	2
1973−1975	66	20	7	5	3
1976−1977	65	17	8	8	2

While almost one out of five respondents in the most recent vintage, 1976-1977, reported that he or she worked more than 20 hours per week either at the time of the survey or at some time during the previous 12 months, only 6 percent of the respondents in the oldest vintage reported working more than 20 hours a week for pay. In general, then, it can be said that while the allocation of hours to major nonpaid work activities does not differ noticeably between younger and older retirees and more recent and older retirement vintages, the same cannot be said about paid work activities. Not only do more recent vintages tend to have a higher rate of work experience and a higher rate of present work status, but they also tend to put in longer hours per week, when they do work for pay.

Of course a far higher proportion of all retirees are engaged to some extent in the major nonpaid work activities we have distinguished than in paid work activities, particularly in such activities as domestic chores, hobbies and recreation, and home maintenace activities. Even volunteer service attracts a much higher proportion of all vintages than does paid work. Although paid work, either in the form of salaried employment, self-employment or consulting work, involves a sizable minority of the retired managers and technical/ professional personnel we have surveyed, it is dwarfed by the total significance of nonpaid activities in the lives of the great majority.

Although there were some minor difference in the degree to which members of the different vintages planned for many of the specific aspects of retirement, the major differences involved planning for either salaried employment, consulting or self-employment. The more recent vintages reported taking more active steps with respect to postretirement work experience than did the earlier vintages. This was particularly the case with the most recent vintage. Almost one out of five of those who retired in 1976–1977 took active steps to secure self-employment or consulting work, compared with only about one out of ten in the older vintages.

Although the extent of planning, with the exception of planning for consulting work or self-employment, was fairly similar for the four vintages, attitudes toward inflation were markedly different. Respondents were asked whether they thought at the time of their retirement that inflation would be under 5 percent, 5 percent or more, or whether they had not given much thought to the matter. Table 5.5 gives the percentage distribution of each vintage with respect ot the three possible answers.

Table 5.5 Retirees' Opinions (at time of retirement) on Future Rate of Inflation (in percent)

Vintage	Thought Inflation Would Be:		Did Not Give It Much Thought
	Under 5 Percent	5 Percent or More	
1968–1969	27	23	50
1970–1972	27	30	44
1973–1975	23	42	36
1976–1977	21	54	26

The oldest vintage retired at the onset of the long period of inflation which began with the Vietnam War. As they recall their attitude toward the matter, one out of two report that they were relatively unconcerned and only one out of four anticipated a high rate of inflation. But even in the case of the most recent vintage, those retiring in 1976–1977, only slightly more than one out of two felt that inflation would be likely to exceed 5 percent per year. Even more surprising, one out of four does not recall giving the matter much thought.

On the other hand, it is clear that a pervasive trend toward giving more attention to inflation and thinking that it will be more severe is revealed by the table. In their comments, the respondents indicate that inflation is now by all odds their most serious concern, the source of their greatest fears and anxieties, indeed in many cases of despair about the future. That such a high proportion of those who retired between 1970 and 1977 should now admit that, as they now recollect the matter, they did not give much thought to an issue which was to upset so much of their financial planning and to cause such anxiety is an occasion for some wonder. These same individuals were in the middle and higher echelons of executive ranks in three major American corporations, and their educational level was conspicuously higher than the national average. Many of them apparently could not believe, at the time of their retirement, that inflation might prove as intractable as it has become. The comments of many indicate a position of disbelief in the capacity and will of the federal government to do anything to lower the rate of inflation.

Although there is little difference in the degree of planning activity among the four vintages, except with respect to planning for self-employment and consulting work, the four vintages used company conseling services somewhat differently. Only three out of ten of the oldest vintage report using such services, while almost one out of two of the most recent vintage used them. This increase in the use of company-provided conseling services was associated with an increasing belief that the services were in fact useful before they were in fact utilized. But after using the services, the four vintages display little difference in their attitude toward the actual usefulness of preretirement counseling.

A somewhat higher proportion of the recent retirees feel that they retired too soon. The most recent vintage are apt to say that they retired too soon because they miss either their work or the social contacts which surrounded their work. Even so, the specter of inflation is the element, along with the behavior of the stock market, common to members of all four vintages who report that they retired too soon.

Another respect in which the respondents of the four vintages differ systematically is in the reasons they give for not being presently at work. While there is little difference in the proportions who say that they are not at work because there is no job opportunity, either in their own field or in any field (about one in six gives this reason), the older vintages are more likely to say that poor health and/or a lack of desire for work are among the reasons for not working.

With respect to the reasons given for initiating a request for retirement, several interesting differences emerged between the oldest and the most recent vintages. Seventy percent of the oldest vintage who had initiated their retirement included among the reasons for their request the fact that they had enough assets. In contrast, slightly less than half of the most recent vintage felt that they had enough assets to retire. On the other hand, only one out of eight of the older vintage reported that retirement was associated with an attractive pension offer, while one out of five of the most recent vintage reported such an offer. The most pervasive and widest differences between the earlier and the more recent vintages, however, centered around attitudes toward working conditions and conflict with superiors. The physical demands of the job, stress of decision-making, difficulties in meeting company expectations, resentment of supervision and conflict with superiors were all more frequently mentioned by the most recent vintage as reasons for electing early retirement. In addition, while three out of ten of the retirees of 1968–1969 gave the statement, "having risen as far as I could within the firm, my job no longer provided the same challenge and satisfaction," as one of the reasons for early retirement, four out of ten of the most recent vintage took this position. Finally, a higher proportion of the most recent retirees stated that they had retired because they had worked long enough. In other words, even though the most recent retirees felt somewhat less financial security in retiring, their dissatisfaction with actual conditions of work seems to have been sufficiently great (as opposed to the earlier retirees) to tip the balance in favor of early retirement.

Nevertheless, it should be emphasized at this point that if such a trade-off did take place, it may be a somewhat more doubtful issue in the future. Heightened inflation and a longer time horizon for inflation will increase the concern of individuals in their late fifties and early sixties whether their financial assets will be adequate to cover what may well prove to be a lengthened life. At the same time, continued high levels of inflation will make it more difficult for companies to "sweeten" pension offers, particularly by providing "inflation guards" for pensions. There is a limit to the degree of work dissatisfaction that can be allowed, particularly in the middle and higher ranks of management, without serious impacts upon the productivity and effectiveness of managerial personnel. In short, it may prove more and more difficult to induce early retirement in the face of financial insecurity and uncertainty.

An examination of the reasons for retirement given by those who did not initiate a request for early retirement also reveals several differences between the oldest and the most recent vintages. Few of the respondents from the oldest vintage who were retired by their companies said that their retirement was caused by any circumstances other than their having reached mandatory retirement age. In the case of the recent vintage, however, a number of respondents said that company-wide or division personnel cuts or company-exercised options caused their retirement.

At least since 1970, the three companies from which our respondents retired required early retirement for managerial and professional/technical personnel fairly infrequently. In the light of recent amendments to the Age Discrimination in Employment Act raising the age at which mandatory retirement is legal from 65 to 70, it is likely that such forced retirement of managerial personnel will become a more common practice. A reexamination of cases in the recent past where selected individuals were required or induced to retire before reaching mandatory retirement age should throw light on the kinds of problems and responses which companies will encounter in the future if they seek to retire selected managerial personnel before they reach age 70. At the same time, it is possible, perhaps even likely, that managerial personnel may be less compliant in the future than in the past when faced with a request by their companies that they retire before they want to, and may be more willing to resort to litigation and other administrative means to delay or prevent forced early retirement.

Age at Retirement

In addition to the differences and commonalties that we have discussed, there are several interesting differences between early and later vintages which are related to demographic and other personal characteristics of the various vintages. For example, there was a perceptible difference in age distribution at retirement of Vintage 1 compared with Vintage 4 (see Table 5.6).

Whereas only one out of seven of the oldest vintage retired before reaching 60 years of age, three out of ten of the most recent vintage elected to retire before 60. The fact that this vintage tended to retire at

Table 5.6 Age at Retirement (percent distribution)

Vintage	54 and Younger	55—59	60—64	65	Total
Vintage 1 1968—1969	0	13	62	25	100
Vintage 4 1976—1977	4	26	55	15	100

somewhat younger ages, combined with their retirement in 1976-1977 rather than 1968-1969, made the age distribution of the most recent vintage at the time of the survey quite different from that of the oldest vintage (see Table 5.7). In the light of the difference in age distribution at the time of the survey, the fact that rates of paid work activity and unpaid activities of the oldest vintage differ so little from those of the most recent vintage take on heightened interest and importance.

Not only were members of the oldest vintage somewhat older at the time of their retirement than were members of the most recent vintage, they also had worked, on the average, for the company from which they retired far more years than had members of the most recent cohort (see Table 5.8).

The decreasing length of job tenure that is associated with recent vintages compared to older vintages tends to confirm the opinion of many personnel administrators of large corporations that managerial and professional/technical personnel at the present time, particularly those in the younger age groups, are more willing to shift from one large corporation to another or to shift their career directions even more drastically.

The long tenure on the jobs of a considerable proportion of our respondents, for many going back to the 1930s or even earlier, may be

Table 5.7 Age at Time of Survey (percent distribution)

Vintage	54 or Under	55—59	60—63	64—67	68 and Over	Total
Vintage 1	0	0	0	8	92	100
Vintage 4	2	19	39	40	0	100

Table 5.8 Years with Company at Retirement (percent distribution)

Vintage	30 or Less	31 to 40	41 and Over	Total
Vintage 1	16	47	37	100
Vintage 4	29	56	15	100

a reflection of a combination of fears generated by the Great Depression of the thirties, fears which made individuals reluctant to quit secure jobs for greener pastures and the satisfactions accompanying promotion for managerial personnel associated with the expansion of major American corporations in the postwar decades.

Increased portability of pension benefits and increasing acceptance by corporations of career paths which include service in a succession of companies may interact to shorten even more in the future the length of job tenure of middle and upper levels of managerial and professional/technical personnel. It may also turn out that managerial personnel whose careers have included several changes of employers will in the future be able to combine early retirement from their principal employer with subsequent work experience because of their greater familiarity with the job market and their decreased anxiety about job searching.

A loosening of career boundaries and a heightened flexibility of options may therefore increase the numbers of individuals who nominally retire in their fifties but who in reality want to substitute a more flexible and looser tie to the world of work and employing institutions for the highly institutionalized relationship between middle and upper levels of management that has been characteristic of many large American corporations. Whether such a development occurs will depend upon how tight the labor market in the next decade turns out to be for the executive who is in or approaching his fifties.

One of the possibly perverse effects of a combination of raising the legal mandatory retirement age to 70 and the high and increasing costs of defined benefit pension plans may be a sharp increase in the unwillingness of some large corporations to hire managerial and professional/technical personnel who are in their forties and fifties. Large national corporations usually have generous pension plans and are reluctant to take actions to dismiss elderly employees for cause which run the risk of costly and unpleasant litigation and damage to the company's public image and the morale of its executive corps.

They can decrease the likelihood of such instances by not hiring middle-aged managerial employees who might often be inclined to remain in their employment through age 70. Firms that are now willing to carry a few employees in their early 60s whose productivity has declined may be much more cautious about carrying a larger number of employees for a longer period of time.

On the other hand, the work experience of our respondents indicates that a considerable proportion of them has remained both active and productive during many years of retirement. The comments of some indicate that the postretirement years have been among the most productive and successful of their lives, releasing hitherto unused capacities and energies. Moreover, most of the respondents indicate that they prefer shorter and more flexible work schedules. How to make the most effective use of the highly motivated, experienced and energetic older managerial employees during their 60s without creating rigid hiring, promotion and dismissal practices which penalize some and afford grounds for charges of discriminatory personnel practices is certain to be one of the challenges of enlightened management in the decades to come.

AGE AT RETIREMENT

We have already remarked that average age at retirement for those electing early retirement decreased between 1968 and 1977. The relationships between (1) work experience during retirement, (2) present work status, (3) satisfaction with retirement, (4) the degree to which actual retirement experiences have conformed to preretirement expectations and age at retirement throw some light upon whether the trend towards early retirement will accelerate or level off.

First of all, were those respondents who retired at a relatively early age more or less satisfied with their retirement experience than those who retired later in their life or at mandatory retirement age? The statistical data are fairly clear cut. Although all age groups are more or less satisfied with retirement, the handful of individuals who retired before age 55 were comparatively very satisfied while those who retired between age 55 and 59 were comparatively less satisfied. Those who retired between age 60 and 64 were comparatively very satisfied, except for age 63. Those who retired at age 65 were somewhat more satisfied than those who retired at age 63.

The reader will recall that many of those who retired at age 63 were in fact mandatorily retired because one of the companies, Chain Store, during part of the period between 1968–1977 set 63 as the age for mandatory retirement. Not only did some of the Chain Store respondents resent being retired at age 63, but a good proportion of them have also felt considerable financial pressure because their retirement income is so heavily dependent upon the performance of Chain Store stock.

The dissatisfactions of Chain Store respondents who were retired mandatorily at age 63 tend to be both understandable and vocal. In sum, it is clear that with the exception of age 63 at retirement (and to a much smaller extent age 65, the age for mandatory retirement for the other two companies), those respondents who were relatively older at the time of their retirement were on the average somewhat more satisfied with their retirement experiences than were those who retired in their late fifties.

We want to emphasize again, however, that most respondents, regardless of their age at retirement, reported that they were more or less satisfied with retirement. A major reversal in the trend toward early retirement of managerial personnel, therefore, will not, in our estimation, come as a result of widespread dissatisfaction with retirement experience, unless the effect of continued and increasingly high rates of inflation so erodes standards of living that both expectations of a satisfactory retirement experience and actual satisfaction with retirement are radically altered.

We have discussed satisfactions with retirement. A related question is whether retirement experiences have more or less conformed to expectations. The pattern that is evident in the case of satisfaction with retirement is more or less duplicated when the degree of fulfillment of retirement expectations is related to age at retirement. Those who were mandatorily retired, either at age 65 or 63, and those who were under 60 when they retired were less likely to report that their retirement experiences have been very similar to what they expected. It should be noted, however, that some of our respondents made specific comments to the effect that their retirement experience had been either much more satisfactory than they had expected or much less.

Most of our respondents did expect that their retirement would be more or less satisfactory, and for most of them their expectations were fairly well met. This was particularly the case for those who elected early retirement in their 60s. It seems that the retirement experiences of those who retired at an even younger age were somewhat more problematic. It may also be that the expectations of those who retired before they reached 60 were somewhat less realistic, and therefore the retiree was more apt to be disappointed by events over which he had insufficient control. Finally, it is also very likely that those retirees who retired before they reached 60 had less resources in the form of pension benefits and accumulated assets and were more alarmed, because of their longer life expectancy, by the prospects of high rates of inflation during the many years that lie before them.

Work experience after retirement is negatively correlated with age at retirement. Half of the relatively few respondents who retired at age 55 or less have had some work experience during retirement, and a similar proportion were either at work at the time of the survey or had worked during the previous 12 months. Similarly high rates of work experience are true of those who were 56 and 57 when they retired. However, after age 58 the rate of work experience during retirement falls rather sharply with increasing age at retirement.

About 50 percent of the respondents who retired in their middle fifties had some work experience during retirement, and almost as large a proportion of them were either working at the time of the survey or had worked at some time in the previous 12 months. Only about one out of three of the respondents who retired when they were about 60 years old had had any work experience, and less than three out of ten were at work at the time of the survey or had worked in the previous 12 months. As for those respondents who retired when they were 64 or 65 years of age, only three out of ten had any postretirement work experience, and only about two out ten respondents who had retired at these ages were at work at the time of the survey or had worked during the previous 12 months.

Of some interest is the fact that respondents who retired either at age 65 or age 63 had somewhat higher rates of present work status than did respondents who had retired when they were one year younger. This was particularly the case for retirement at age 63. Only a quarter of respondents who retired at age 62 were working at the time of the survey or had worked during the past 12 months. In contrast, almost a third of the respondents who retired at age 63 reported that they were working or had worked at some time during the previous 12 months. These higher rates of present work status were undoubtedly a result of the fact that a considerable proportion of the respondents who retired at age 63 and 65 were mandatorily retired.

Age at the Time of the Survey

We have already had occasion to call attention to the fact that levels of nonwork activity remained high throughout the retirement experience for most of our respondents, regardless of age. The exception to this generalization was a relatively small group whose health situations made for major decreases in the amount of time devoted to activities in which good health is at a premium.

High levels of activity regardless of age are somewhat less evident in the case of time devoted to work activity. Not only does the amount of time spent per week decrease fairly steadily with age, the proportion of respondents in the higher age brackets who at the time of the survey were working or had worked during the previous 12 months was markedly lower than was the case for the younger age brackets.

The contrast between rates of work experience during retirement by age and rates of present work status by age is revealing:

Table 5.9   Rates of Work Experience during Retirement and
Present Work Status (in percent)

Age Group	With Work Experience during Retirement	At Work at Time of Survey or during Previous 12 Months
54–61	46	43
62–65	41	36
66–69	33	23
70 or over	32	22

For the younger age groups, 54-61 and 62-65, there is little difference between the proportion who were at work at the time of the survey or at some time during the previous 12 months and the proportion who had some work experience during retirement. For the two older age groups, however, there is a distinct difference between the two, indicating that many of the older retirees gave up work activity when they reached age 66–69. Even so, about one out of five of the group aged 70 or over reported that they were at work at the time of the survey or had worked at some time in the previous 12 months.

Examination of types of work activity by age reveals that the older retirees tended to be engaged in self-employment or consulting work rather than salaried employment. Whether this is because self-employment and consulting work permit a retiree to work longer years, the reason many of them gave when they were asked why they chose these types of work activity, or whether self-employment and consulting work are more suited to the shorter and more flexible work schedules preferred by the older retirees is an open question.

It should be recalled, however, that members of the most recent vintage, the retirees of 1976–1977, indicated a strong preference for consulting work and self-employment along with a high degree of satisfaction with such postretirement work activity. The choice of these two kinds of work activity may indicate that many of the recent and prospective early retirees hope and intend to work for as long as possible during their retirement. It may also indicate that a large pool of managerial and professional/technical talent will be available in the future to those corporations that develop procedures to encourage retirees to work as consultants or to provide services to the corporation as self-employed individuals.

The Retirement Experience of Women Respondents

Some interesting differences emerged between the male and female retirees in our sample. But since there were only 48 females in our sample, any patterns which appear should be evaluated cautiously. Furthermore, a large proportion of the females was from one of the corporations, the Utility. Indeed, the Manufacturing corporation had only one female respondent out of the more than 400 retirees from this corporation who responded.

Females were distributed in their preretirement careers differently than were males. Although both men and women were more likely to be managers than professional or technical personnel, females were even more likely than males to have been managers (75 percent compared with 62 percent male). Women were also underrepresented in sales and marketing, and somewhat overrepresented in the "other" category which indicates a high involvement in various ancillary corporate services.

Women were also more likely to fall in the lower end of the salary range. In the year before retirement, 64 percent made less than $24,000, compared to 34 percent of the males. Only one made $30,000 or more, compared to 33 percent of the men. The total family income of women in the year before retirement was also on the average lower than that of men, particularly since many of the women were single. Less than half of the women respondents were married, either in the year before retirement or in the présent, whereas almost all of the men were married. In the case of those women respondents who were married, total family income was somewhat higher than the average for all respondents. Because male salaries after retirement contributed to total family income to a greater extent, females in retirement tended to rely a bit more heavily than males on investment income.

Part of the reason for income differences between men and women in our sample may have arisen from educational differences. Males in general were better educated: a larger proportion graduated from college and subsequently received some kind of advanced training. Females were also somewhat younger when they retired, and in general they were more recently retired. Half of the females were under 60 at the time of retirement, compared to less than a fourth of the men. Similarly, about four out of five had retired within the last five years, compared to only about half of the men. Women obviously had not obtained positions at the career levels used in our study in any significant numbers in time to enable them to retire in the late 1960s or the early 1970s. The length of job tenure for women was also somewhat shorter than that of men, although the majority of both males and females had been with their company for more than 30 years at their retirement.

While our women respondents were working with their company, they were much more likely to work a conventional 40-hour week than males, many of whom put in much longer hours, probably because their higher job status and level of responsibility demanded it.

Males and females retired for different reasons. Eighty-five percent of the females initiated their own retirement, compared to 65 percent of the males. A majority of both males and females said that they had initiated their retirement in part because they had enough assets to enable them to retire. Males, however, were more likely to give this as one of their reasons for retirement and were also more likely to say that they had received an attractive pension offer, or an offer from another company, or that they wanted to start consulting work or enter self-employment. Men were also more likely to complain about health concerns (25 percent to 17 percent) and to call attention to problems of stress at their work (16 percent to 7 percent). Men also said more often than women that their job had lost its challenge and more frequently gave conflicts with their superiors as one of the reasons for retirement. They also asserted more frequently that high taxes had reduced the incentive to continue working. Women, on the other hand, were more likely to say that they retired among other reasons because they had worked long enough, in spite of the fact that on the average they were younger than men at retirement and had worked fewer years with their companies.

There were also differences between males and females among those who did not initiate their retirement. Women tended not to be forced out by company reorganizations or interpersonal conflicts. No woman cited company-wide cuts, divisional or departmental re- ductions in staff, company options or conflicts with superiors, whereas these causes for nonself-initiated retirement were mentioned by small numbers of men (never more than 10 percent of those who did not initiate their own retirement, most of whom were in fact retired because of mandatory retirement provisions).

Men and women planned for retirement in different ways as well. Although both groups used company counseling in approximately equal proportions, females found the counseling services somewhat more useful. Females who did not use company services were more hesitant to discuss personal aspects of their lives with company- provided counselors. Males, on the other hand, were more likely to be unaware that their company provided counseling services.

Both men and women had similar feelings about the timing of their retirement. About a fifth of each group felt that they had retired too soon. Men more often cited financial reasons for their attitude (inflation or the adverse behavior of the stock market). Women more often cited social reasons or said that they found too much un- stimulating time on their hands. Women were apt to say that they missed contacts with people, did not have enough to do, and regretted no longer having the challenge of their jobs.

Although women were somewhat less likely than men to be careful planners for their retirement, they were somewhat more likely to say that their retirement experiences did not meet their expectations, and they were somewhat less satisfied with their retirement life. It will be recalled that the "careful planners" were most apt to be surprised by their actual retirement experiences and to be disappointed. It appears that the disappointed "careful planners" tended to be men; it can be surmised that these were individuals who had tended to assert a considerable degree of control over their environment and their career progress and who had attempted to carry the kind of careful planning

associated with their work careers into their retirement years, when
objective circumstances made it more difficult for them to control
their environment to the same extent or to contend with personal
factors as completely. The women among our respondents did not
seem to make these kinds of demands upon their environment or
themselves as frequently or strenuously. They also seem to have had a
somewhat shorter time horizon in their planning.

Males, for example, were likely to know their retirement date for a
longer period of time and were more likely to take active steps to
secure salaried employment or some other form of postretirement
paid work, as well as to plan more carefully their investments and
postretirement travel. Males were more likely to have thought about
the rate of inflation. Seventy percent of the women said that they had
not given the rate of inflation much thought at the time of their
retirement (it should be recalled that most of our women respondents
retired during the last five years). Less than 40 percent of the men who
retired during these same years reported that they had not given much
thought to inflation. Those women who did give some thought to
inflation, however, were more likely than men to estimate that the
rate of inflation would be more than 5 percent.

An area in which women were conspicuously more careful planners than men concerned planning for their spouses' retirement at the
time of their own. Most of the men in our sample did not have
working wives. Females were more likely to time their retirement for
the approximate date of their spouse's retirement. And in their
comments about retirement, several of the women respondents
expressed resentment or regret that their own careers had to be
terminated in part because their husband's retirement and plans to
relocate made it impossible for them to continue their own career.

Planning did have an effect upon actual retirement experiences.
More males than females were working for pay, and males were more
likely to have continuous work experience since retirement. Of those
who were working for an employer, men were more likely to work for
larger-sized firms and to be doing work similar to their preretirement
job. Men were also much more likely to be self-employed. Practically
no women were engaged in consulting work during retirement.

Of those who felt that they were in the wrong kind of work before
retirement and wanted to continue to work after retirement, men were
more likely to be able to make the change after retirement into new
and unusual careers, such as professional fishermen, whereas women
were more likely to be stuck in routine work and to express dis-

satisfaction both with the kind of work available and with the lack of employment opportunities.

A relatively high proportion of both men and women obtained their postretirement salaried employment before they retired or within a month afterwards. Still, one out of four men said that they had looked for employment for more than a month. Women seem to have been somewhat less willing to search for postretirement salaried employment for any length of time. Females who did not find a job right away may have given up looking without great disappointment or regret, whereas older males may have felt that their self-image depended upon finding work; and they may have been willing to persist in their job search somewhat longer. Another reason for the somewhat longer job search patterns of men may be the greater choosiness on the part of men about the type of work ultimately accepted.

An indication of the better opportunities which may be available to males if they persist in their search is that the employed males were more satisfied with their postretirement job than were females. This higher rate of job satisfaction exists in spite of the fact that employed males were less likely to have the type of work schedule they preferred. Although males were more likely than females to say that they preferred part-time, part-year schedules, employed males were more likely to be working full time for either the whole year or part of the year, whereas females were more likely to be working the part-time, part-year schedules that males prefer.

Of those women and men who chose not to work after retirement, women were more likely to say that they no longer wished to work. This seems to be closely related to their saying more often than men that they retired because they had worked long enough. On the other hand, men who chose not to work were much more likely to say that the reason for their nonwork status was the lack of sufficient economic incentives after taxes. Men who were not working often, in their comments, called particular attention to the disincentive effects of Social Security income limitations and expressed great resentment about both the effect of these limitations and their injustice.

Females after retirement spend more time in unpaid activities of a wide range. Sixty-four percent of the women respondents spend more than 40 hours a week in unpaid activities, compared to 42 percent of the males. Only 11 percent of the women spend 25 hours or less, compared to 28 percent of the males. The pattern was fairly similar for volunteer work, hobbies and recreation, and routine domestic chores. Males, however, as might be expected, spend much more time in home maintenance, which for many of the male respondents clearly served as a partial substitute for their preretirement work, both as a means of releasing energies and of obtaining a feeling of satisfaction from accomplishing a task.

June Stanton is a fairly typical example of females who responded to our questionnaire. She retired in 1975 on her own initiative at the age of 57 after 35 years working for the Utility in administration and personnel management. Her husband had not wished her to work any longer since he was retiring. She currently spends the bulk of her time each week at hobbies and recreation and in routine domestic chores. After retirement, she and her husband moved more than a thousand miles to a village whose residents were mainly retired persons, although it is not strictly a retirement community. Because of inflation's effect upon the family income, she feels that she retired too soon. But she also misses keenly the social contacts of her job and the challenges of her preretirement work. Although she did some planning for her retirement, retirement has not met her expectations fully and she expresses some degree of disappointment and dissatisfaction. Mrs. Stanton finds her income limiting, her social life unsatisfying, and her health poor. Whereas her income was $24,000 in the year before retirement, she currently has no earnings and total family income has decreased from $35,000 to $11,000. Out of her moderate dissatisfaction with retirement she writes:

> Upon retirement I moved (with my husband) to a small village on a huge lake with many facilities for fishing, hunting, and hiking. We are 100 miles from a city of any size. We miss the advantages a large city offers: good medical care, adult education, cultural advantages and shops. There are practically no opportunities away from large cities to use past training and experience in either the employment market or voluntary services. The only problem I ran into in seeking employment in a nearby (4,000 population) town was being considered over-qualified . . . I enjoyed many years of challenging employment with my company and regretted retiring early. (#793)

6

The Retirement Decision in Retrospect: A Distillation of Comments

Comments made about retirement in retrospect reflected a variety of attitudes toward retirement, national and corporate policy, and the financial and social position of the retiree. Approximately one-third of our respondents wrote extensively, and since they were asked to make comments or recommendations about (1) postretirement employment, (2) company pensions and retirement policies, and (3) national policies concerning retirement, age discrimination and social security, responses clustered around these topics.

Degree of Satisfaction and Postretirement Employment

Attitudes expressed in comments at the end of the questionnaire were a reflection of respondents' life situations as portrayed in the more structured part of the questionnaire and ranged from extreme satisfaction to extreme dissatisfaction. Most of the retirees in our sample were satisfied, although a large number qualified their satisfaction, as mentioned earlier. The following is a typical comment by a male retiree who worked in research and development for 32 years before retiring five years ago at the age of 65, who continued to work earning a family income of $16,000:

Having been retired, I tried to adjust to that leisure life but found it increasingly difficult to cope with so much free time.

Fortunately for me, a new program was being developed in my area as a service to the elderly. I applied and was hired to one of the administrative positions. It has turned out to be one of the most satisfying positions I have held. . . .

I see accomplishments, not in the abstract as before, but in the real person-to-person form of satisfaction. In this area I have helped to resolve for other retirees the problems encountered after retirement. (#310)

A Male Chain Store retiree who worked in administration for 37 years before retiring three years ago at the age of 62, who continues to be employed on salary in a different job with a family income of $100,000 commented:

I believe everyone owes himself a second career. They should retire early (60-65) and launch a new career utilizing their talents in a somewhat different direction or profession in order to enjoy life at its fullest. (#2)

A male Chain Store retiree who worked in sales and marketing for 26 years before retiring in 1968 at the age of 55, with a present family income of $18,000, pointed out the challenge of learning new activity and testing new abilities at a late age. He is presently self-employed:

With my limited formal education I was challenged with the thought of being capable of doing something other than merchandise—having worked only for Penney's and Chain Store—also I was concerned over having nothing to do at retirement if I waited until mandatory age 65.

Learning anew at my age was tough—but very gratifying to find I could soon accomplish above average in a relatively short time. My new field is insurance and financial services. Also I have had a long-consuming desire to become more knowledgeable of our Bible. This too has been an absorbing interest and gratifying. I now teach quite often in our church school, and this is a source of real joy in my life. (#371)

Those who expressed satisfaction through postretirement employment sometimes had new jobs that were quite different from their preretirement careers. These were sometimes the outgrowth of preretirement hobbies, as in the following comment by a male Chain

Store retiree who had spent 27 years in sales and marketing before retiring at the age of 55, with a present family income of $20,000:

Can only say my avocation (dancing and teaching dancing part time to professional-type people in private clubs such as Elks, golf clubs, yacht clubs, etc., and aboard cruise ships as exercise leader, dance teacher and staff work) was available and for eight years have taken advantage of it. Would have done something else active if not this. After 27 years I was very happy to pursue other activities. Have had many other opportunities to work but was not interested in a 40-hour job again. Did have a Real Estate Insurance and Security license after retirement but decided I did not want to devote the time necessary to make it successful. Also had many opportunities for club management. (#380)

Several had become fishermen or were involved with ranches or farms. A rancher who had worked for 20 years in sales and marketing before retiring in 1970 at age 68 writes:

Do not care to sit down and die as all my friends have who were mostly bankers.

At 75 years of age spent most of last winter caring for 500 herd of cattle and 400 head of hogs. So am in good health and willing to put in a day's work. (#499)

One of our respondents went into politics after retirement. Another returned to school and became a college psychology instructor. Still another became a priest.

The above respondents emphasize satisfaction with postretirement employment. As mentioned earlier, however, employment was only one way of structuring one's time after retirement. Not all of those who were leading fairly structured lives after retirement were necessarily employed or spending a large number of hours per week engaged in work for pay. The following respondents typify those who were extremely satisfied and who, although not working for pay, used their hobbies and recreation or their volunteer work as a structured and regular activity pattern. A male Manufacturing retiree, who retired in 1971 at age 61 after 41 years in research and development and production, comments:

As for me, I wonder how I ever would find time to go to work (paid), as I'm so busy working for nursing home committees, health organization board of directors, trustee for a hospital, treasurer of church, state church board of directors, etc. (#394)

A male who worked for Utility in sales and marketing for 30 years before his retirement two years ago at the age of 60, with a present family income of $18,000, writes of his high involvement in a structured fashion with his hobbies:

For me, retirement was a joy and a reward for working hard 48 years. It was a realization of a great desire on my part to pursue the many interests that I had little time for during my working years.

I now spend as many hours working each day as I always did, but on the hobbies I never had time for during my working years. I feel sorry for people who think that compulsory retirement should be changed to age 70 or eliminated altogether, but if this is what they want, why not? (#586)

One respondent, a male Utility retiree with a family income of $51,000, who worked in sales and marketing for 37 years before his retirement in 1973 at the age of 62, attached a printed card which indicated his time allocation to various activities after retirement, including some time spent working for pay, which was not, however, a central activity. He had passed them out to all associates and friends upon retiring:

Retirement Plans

Traveling & Socializing	25%
Family Concerns	20%
Home Improvements and Maintenance	20%
Sniffing Out Opportunities to Supplement Pension	15%
Community Activities	10%
Noncommitted	10%

(#852)

Not all of those who were active after retirement in nonwork-related activities necessarily imposed a work-oriented structure upon those activities. The following respondent, although describing a rather active life, does not appear to have arranged her activities into a pattern resembling a 40-hour workweek. She had been an accountant for the Utility for 40 years before retiring in 1974 at age 59.

I worked for 40 years and enjoyed my work. I retired because there were so many things I had never been able to do because there was no time. Now I can play bridge, raise flowers (I always did), cook and entertain. Take a trip when it's not a weekend. Belong to church altar guild and daytime church groups. Take regular college courses instead of at night—I'm not interested in a degree but there is a college in my neighborhood and I enroll for subjects that interest me.

My retirement life is very busy—I probably try to crowd too much in and have frequent conflicts. (#892)

Extreme satisfaction was also expressed by some whose postretirement lives had been less active and/or even less structured. The following respondent typifies the unstructured positive adaptability to retirement. Since he is no longer working, but rather traveling and engaged in lake recreation, the underlying work ethic in our culture leads him to be somewhat defensive about his activities. A Manufacturing retiree with a present family income of $10,000, who worked for 28 years in both production and research and development before his retirement in 1976 at the age of 60, he writes:

As I look at my answers I can see where I might be considered lazy, antisocial, and other things. (#388)

A male Manufacturing retiree with a present family income of $30,000, who spent 43 years in research and development before retiring 10 years ago at the age of 65, comments:

Being a believer in C. P. Snow's concept of a two-culture world and having devoted most of my life to the technologies, I decided to concentrate on the humanities after retirement. Accordingly, my wife and I have spent considerable time in foreign travel, visiting art galleries and studying art history. In connection with the travel I have attempted to acquire a smattering of the language of the country involved.

It is my feeling that one should have two kinds of hobbies upon which to expand after retirement—some involving physical activity and others requiring thoughtful concentration and mental effort. Should physical activity become difficult, there remains plenty to occupy one's time profitably and very possibly with benefit to others.

I have particularly enjoyed living with a minimum of structured time and pressure to meet deadlines. Very selfishly, we have liked doing what we want to, rather than what someone else might want us to do. (#645)

Some respondents became very contemplative after retirement, placing even less emphasis on physical activity than the above respondent. One retiree from the Utility who had spent 43 years in engineering and economics retired in 1972 at age 62. He offers this reflection:

The holistic development of our complete (real) selves is the major job of our twilight years. You are always asked what are you "doing" in your retirement—strangely no one asks what are you thinking about. What grabs you mentally—that is what counts. (#920)

A large number of our respondents were satisfied overall but with qualifications, as illustrated in the following comment by a male Chain Store retiree, involved in sales and marketing for 25 years before his retirement at age 63 six years ago. His present family income is $35,000 and he is presently not working for pay:

Financially, I was not ready for retirement in 1972. I had been at Chain Store only 25 years, so retirement benefits were not quite up to my needs. I wanted to work three more years and was fortunate enough to have a job opportunity at more salary than I had made at Chain Store.

I now enjoy the freedom for travel, time for hobbies and time for attention to investments. (Keeping up with inflation is a real problem.)

After retiring for the second time two years ago, however, I now feel an ideal situation would be to have a one-day-a-week job (with pay), provided it would be both pleasant and stimulating—and it would have to be with freedom to leave for periods of travel. Such a job would give me a feeling of involvement plus supplementing my income. Such a job is not easy to find, of course, due primarily to my requirement for freedom to take time off. (#89)

A financial analyst for the Utility makes the following observation:

If one is to say that "retirement years are for enjoyment in the twilight years of one's life after a life-long contribution to industry and society," then it must also be said that society at the very least owes a retired person the right to live in dignity, free from erosion of savings by taxes and inflation.

On the brighter side I find that retirement has given me a large measure of satisfaction in being able to do the things I want to do when I want to do them. It is almost imperative for a person contemplating retirement to acquire hobbies or other diversions. (#180)

A male Utility retiree, working in production for 38 years before his retirement 10 years ago at the age of 62, presently not working for pay and with an unrevealed present income, wrote:

In a period of approximately two years, my wife and I were often hospitalized, limiting our social life. At present my wife is gradually approaching invalidism. I have dedicated myself to help her, and do all the housework; however, I do have a cleaning person every other week.

The first five years after retirement we did enjoy ourselves by travel, fishing up north, and visiting our two children and their families. During this time we had a home in Florida that required considerable work. However, we did enjoy the home, community and that kind of living. When these activities seemed to be too much with our health getting worse, we moved into a condominium. (#210)

Ambivalence about the degree of satisfaction with one's retirement often centered around insufficient finances or health problems of self or a family member, as in the above case. Extreme dissatisfaction also tended to be paired with financial problems and poor health, as well as bitterness about no longer being considered potentially useful. A woman who had worked for 33 years for Chain Store retired at age 60 in 1975 when her family income was $25,000. It is now $9,000 and she has second thoughts:

If I had known the feelings of despair in not having a job and not getting a salary each week, I would have thought twice about "early" retirement. I live in a community where there is little opportunity for employment, much less in the field in which I was employed. I do some volunteer work for the church, but it is not as fulfilling as I would like it to be. When one has to think twice when purchasing food or clothing due to the price one cannot afford, it is frustrating. Only reason I did retire was because my husband had reached his retirement age and wanted to leave the "Big City." (#496)

A Manufacturing retiree who refused to fill in the structured part of the questionnaire wrote:

The vicissitudes of life have two "apocalyptic horses"—senescense and disease . . . The *returning traveler* has no place in society. He has no "story" to tell. Furthermore, in a society where physical strength is glorified to its maximum possible height—next to possession of wealth—the aged and those aging are natural outcasts. The spectacle of old people dancing, trotting, etc., is ludicrous.

I retired to recover my health and to start a new way of work, and in a professionally new field. Have failed on both counts. Was refused, I naturally believe unjustly, dissability "status." (#98)

Paid work but only at a better-than-menial job was often synonymous with productivity and a sense of being useful to some respondents, who referred to any other status as not on "active duty," and who wished to do more than bag groceries in Florida.

Some respondents expressed dissatisfaction about being forced into early retirement and then forgotten. For example, a male Utility retiree with an unrevealed present income and presently not working, who retired two years ago at the age of 58 after 41 years in production, complained:

My greatest disappointment with retirement is you may as well die, as far as interest by active employees of all levels is concerned. (#734)

Or, from a male Manufacturing retiree presently not working, with a present family income of $29,000, who retired three years ago at the age of 61 after 40 years in sales and marketing:

At the time of your retirement you are the most important man on earth—retirement party, speeches, etc. The next day you are forgotten—you get only the company newspaper but no news of your former department or division—unless you seek it out by calling at the office. (#780)

Those who initiated their own retirement were more likely to say that they were very satisfied with it. In addition, those who were satisfied with their retirement often pointed out that they did not feel ignored by their company. A Manufacturing retiree writes:

I retired at 62 because it seemed to be the right time. After 30 years it looked like the time had come to sit back and rest.

Two days before retirement I had a job offer at a substantial raise in pay and benefits. This I turned down, since money alone cannot be allowed to rule one's life.

After a winter of play in the South I was recalled to my company to assist in a problem. This short term of employment was welcome. I saw old friends and attained a feeling of accomplishment.

The second year I was asked to help again and did so for a short period of time.

Last year I had an urgent request to return from the South and help again. This time I found it necessary to refuse since I had a southern home under reconstruction and could not easily leave . . .

It is wonderful to be needed—either by the company from which you retire or by your family and friends. I have been blessed in every way. (#489)

In general, although we had only a small number of females in our sample (5 percent), they were more likely to be dissatisfied with retirement. Retirees with a greater amount of education were more likely to have greater satisfaction, perhaps because greater alternate uses of time were available to those with broader interests.

A retiree's relationship to his former company and his attitude toward their pension and retirement policies was also often an important source of satisfaction or dissatisfaction with retirement. Respondents tended to voice complaints, more than satisfactions, in these areas.

Company Pensions and Retirement Policies: Causes for Complaints

Of the three corporations included in our study, Chain Store respondents were least satisfied with their present financial condition, even those with fairly substantial incomes. (Still, a majority of Chain Store respondents expressed great or moderate satisfaction.) Dissatisfaction generally focused on the retiree's holdings of the company's stock. A male retiree presently not working for pay, who retired in 1972 at the age of 63 after 32 years in sales and marketing, with a present family income of $22,100, down from $24,900 in the year before retirement, complained:

We really had no company-provided professional counseling in planning retirement. In fact, I was brain-washed through periodic company meetings and showing of films that it was foolish to take any other action than what I took—to keep my stock and not sell! As I look back over 30 years this was true, and for one year after my retirement. During the 30+ years there were stock reverses, but none ever lasted more than a little over three years before a new high was reached. But today it's a different story, and where it will end is anyone's guess.

I don't know how many retirees Chain Store has, but being one of the giants of industry and community leaders, would it be expecting too much for them to do something for those who took the stock and have suffered such great loss in the value of their stock? Other large corporations have done something for their retirees. (#668)

In order to avoid capital gains taxes, many Chain Store respondents feel compelled to hold onto the stock which is the foundation for their retirement income, even though it is decreasing in market value. Their reluctance to sell stock in order to supplement their income from stock dividends and Social Security in many cases has led to a radical reduction in their standard of living. One Chain Store individual, who was able to maintain a family income of $17,000 in the past year only through stock sales and the addition of Social Security, indicated in reference to his financial hardship: "I hope I don't live to be in my nineties."

Not all Chain Store retirees complained about their financial situation. As mentioned above, most were fairly satisfied. The following respondent, a male, 35 years in personnel, who retired nine years ago at the age of 59 with a dip in family income from $35,000 to $18,000 and presently not working for pay, felt Chain Store retirement benefits to be quite liberal.

Chain Store is an excellent employer. Because of its liberal retiree benefits, including financial, I was able to retire when I wanted to, young enough to enjoy a change of pace. I enjoyed my work but I am enjoying retirement more. I am sorry for people who, except for financial reasons, feel that they must "die with their boots on." This comment of course will not apply to volunteer work. (#84)

However, compliments about Chain Store's original retirement benefit plan were the exception rather than the rule.

Chain Store individuals were not the only ones to make complaints about their financial situation. Resentment was generally voiced about the relatively small size of regular private pensions compared to government pensions. A Manufacturing retiree, 32 years in research and development, retired six years ago at the age of 60. His family income had fallen from $25,000 in the year before retirement to $16,000 in the past year, in spite of the fact that he had been self-employed and acting as a consultant on a part-time basis. He complained:

Much ado was made about the pension system as being larger than other companies. This is not true, and the Manufacturing pension tends to look meager against state and federal and even large-city pensions. Publicity of this sort should be realistic to help the retiree in his planning. (#156)

And a male Manufacturing retiree who had worked 32 years in industrial relations to retire in 1972 at the age of 62 with a family income dip from $45,000 before retirement to $21,000 in the past year, partially attained by self-employment and consulting, reasons:

Retirement is unquestionably a tremendous opportunity to be on a prolonged vacation—do what you want when you want to. However, my own feelings are [that] you must be financially able to carry on in hopefully about the same manner as before retirement. My pension with 32 years' service is 22 percent of my final salary, or approximately $6,000 a year. Social Security adds $3,600 more. So now $9,600 has to replace some $26,000. Admittedly taxes are not as large and therefore the cash differential is not so great. It is very difficult to have city, county, state and federal employees retiring at 80 percent of their last three years' pay, knowing what we get and knowing we contribute to the 80 percent. (#722)

Inflation was a very common cause for concern, and many felt cost-of-living adjustment features or tax exemption features should be built into all pensions. One Manufacturing retiree, presently 72 years of age and not working for pay, who had retired eight years ago after 34 years in both production and research and development, with a present family income of $23,000, down from $30,000 in 1969, had taken some steps to ameliorate the problem as he saw it:

I, as a senior citizen, wish to say that no single group than us has suffered more from the effects of big government spending and double-digit inflation. Daily inflation depletes our meager savings, retirement benefits, and pensions. The odds we face are sometimes overwhelming—large medical bills, soaring food and fuel prices, taxes, exorbitant rents, and small Social Security increases that always seem to lag behind. I have convinced my congressman to introduce legislation to ease our financial burden. Bill HR 4278 was issued which would provide for a basic $5,000 income tax exemption for pensions, annuities, or other retirement benefits. This bill is in Ways and Means, and the Honorable Al Ullman has received many thousands of letters, but we have not been able to get it out of committee since 94th Congress and a new bill has been introduced for the 95th which we are working on. I am happy to report we are exempt from income tax on pensions and annuities in my state. (#260)

Postretirement changes in health coverage often added to the financial difficulties of retirees. A Manufacturing employee retired in 1975 at the age of 65 after 39 years in research and development. His family income has fallen from $20,000 to $12,000 and, although he is not working for pay now, he views the future with great misgiving:

I have lived a life which is considered normally American. We raised two children who completed college, which I paid for in entirety. We provided a horse for one and music lessons for the other. We enjoyed a new but modest home, a travel/trailer and a boat.

During this time my spouse worked very little for wages, mostly, when the children were grown, for therapeutic reasons.

Now we have reached mandatory retirement in better than normal health and find we are forced to leave the things we were accustomed to and look forward to finishing off our life in a nursing home as state wards when we can no longer take care of ourselves physically. The reaons are simple:

a) Medical insurance plans do not cover a person as well in retirement as when working. This can be accomplished but the premiums are unaffordable.

b) Pensions erode with inflation in spite of some adjustment.

c) Income generally is much less after retirement.

d) Industrial pensions are less than those provided for government and state employees, yet have been paid for by taxes of the industrial worker.

I'm of the opinion that no person has the right to expect a higher standard of living after retirement than he enjoyed during his working years, unless he has provided it. However, he should not be forced into a regressive standard of living. (#487)

Some respondents, however, felt they were relatively secure financially. One male Utility retiree, for example, presently not working for pay, with a family income of $30,000, down from a 1975 income of $33,000, the year before retirement at age 65 after 47 years in engineering, writes:

From the time of my initial employment the company emphasized that any pension to be received should not be considered adequate to satisfy one's future needs. They advocated employee savings and participation in the purchase of the company's stock. I followed their suggestions—consequently I do not have financial problems at this time or expect any in the forseeable future. In addition, my company continues to exhibit a continuing concern in my existence! (#A41)

On the other hand, another male Chain Store retiree with a family income in the past year of $7,000, a very large decrease from a 1970 income of $16,000, who retired seven years ago at the age of 59 after 30 years as a control buyer, also downplayed problems with finances:

When we retired it was not with the idea of making money at some other form of employment. Rather we sought some means of satisfying our desire to be of service and at the same time have some interest to keep up occupied and active. To this end we moved to a farm where we have a few beef cattle, mainly supplying our needs and those of our daughters' families. We raise vegetables and fruit which we eat fresh and process for use during the rest of the year.

With a little hired help we built a new house and hope to remodel the old one which we moved to an adjoining tract of land. We are able to give more time to our church, find time for other hobbies and still be free to entertain all who come to us, friends, strangers, groups on retreat, and family, especially grandchildren. And added to that is time for reading, meditation or just watching birds, deer, sunrises and sunsets, and the moon coming over the hills, etc. Even with inflation, life is still not necessarily a battle of dollars and cents. There is a challenge

and a satisfaction in knowing we have been able to cope thus far
and find joy and peace in doing it. (#A52)

Finances, however, were not the only source of complaints about
companies. Other complaints about company retirement policies
included the general inflexibility of the corporation in having no
provisions to enable a worker to taper off working gradually and
make a slower and smoother transition into retirement. One retiree,
for example, a male former Manufacturing employee who spent 42
years in research and development before retiring in 1970 at the age of
62, who is currently not working for pay and has a family income of
$20,000, comments:

The "retirement years" expectancy has increased very much in
the past 25 years. Too much valuable manpower is idle. There is
a great need for "tapering off" jobs for "partial retirement."
Adult fun and games and "Golden Age" activities are empty and
contribute to a waste of human resources.
    The increasing need for productivity in all our institutions—
private and public—might well involve retired people on a
reduced-time basis. (#93)

And a female who retired from the Utility when she was 59 writes:

After devoting so many years to working, it is difficult to adjust
to a new lifestyle—particularly because it's so abrupt. If one
could taper off (or diminish the number of days worked) with a
lighter work load and responsibilities, one could develop
psychologically to the adjustments both financially and leisure-
ly. In my situation, it was traumatic (due to a medical problem).
I planned to work until retirement age. (#760)

Many felt they could have been useful to their company on a
consulting or part-time basis. A Manufacturing retiree who retired at
age 60 and whose family income is now $32,000 states:

I would have been glad to work part time, would even now but
there was and is still an age barrier. I firmly believe companies
should strive to allow tapering off to keep personnel working
up to 70, or even longer, ability considered. An "age" as 65 or 70
may be easier to administer, but is "not logical." Manufacturing
did not permit me a three-day week, altho I offered to work five
or six days, if really needed. (#104)

Some respondents had been generally satisfied about their corporate careers but became bitter about the treatment they received in their company the last few years before retirement. A Manufacturing retiree after 30 years in salary and wage administration and union relations, whose present family income is $11,000, declares:

I am extremely resentful of the treatment I received during the last four years I worked for the company, so much so that I will not return to my place of employment. (#357)

Some felt discriminated against, largely because of their age, and forced out. For those who wished to continue working, the feeling was that "they don't hire grey hair." (#58)

There were several comments about management's present attitude. The feeling was that management in large corporations has recently become depersonalized. A retiree from the Utility, after 41 years in production, whose current family income is $40,000, says:

Management has changed in perspective. People don't have the same consideration any longer. Individuality has been forgotten. We were people-oriented. Today this doesn't seem true ... if I had been more political and less direct in my approaches I would have made it. I'm not sorry for up until I left, I enjoyed working. A year or so before my retirement, I got bored with my job and felt it best for the company and myself to get out. When one can get along like a robot without having to think and still do a satisfactory job it isn't fair to the company or the individual to stay around. (#899)

It was also felt that in case of a grievance, there was no means for launching an appeal. One retiree, in sales and marketing for the Manufacturer for 38 years, makes this suggestion:

I retired two years earlier than planned. I feel that the option given me of early retirement or a job with humiliation and less status really left me no choice. I had always done a good job, and I was surprised and hurt by the fact that my immediate superiors were able to get rid of my so easily and put one of "their boys" in my place. I feel that an appeal mechanism, as a routine matter, should cover all cases of "early retirement." (#277)

Overall, although most respondents appear to be satisfied with their retirement and to have positive attitudes toward the corporations they retired from, the comments section of the questionnaire was used to air specific grievances. Experiences with one's company can turn bitter immediately before retirement or in the adjustment period after. Recommendations for company policies oriented toward this problem will be outlined in the final chapter of this book.

Specific grievances concerning national policy were also aired in the comments section of the questionnaire.

National Policies

In spite of the reluctance of some respondents to retire and the subsequent dissatisfaction of some who were forced to, the overwhelming thrust of the reaction to raising the mandatory retirement ceiling was surprisingly negative. Reasons for opposing a raised retirement ceiling often appeared to be grounded in equity. Many felt that retirement at a later age would prevent youth from obtaining jobs. A retiree from the Manufacturer, after 47 years with his company, expresses this concern about youth unemployment:

With high unemployment in the country, it's best to put youth to work. The national policy allowing persons to work until age 70 is a mistake. Social Security earned-income restrictions are in order to give the youth the opportunity to work. (#402)

And a Chain Store retiree is concerned both about efficiency and equity. He retired at age 58 and has a present family income of $55,000.

Legislation banning forced retirement at 65, in my opinion, is a mistake. The older employees should "get out" and give the younger employees an opportunity. Also, many employees 65 and over should not be working. They are less efficient, etc., and are a liability to the employer. (#116)

Others felt that raising the mandatory retirement ceiling would be physically and emotionally damaging to older workers. A Chain Store retiree whose present family income is $11,000 declares:

I personally favor mandatory retirement and feel that 65 is a reasonable age because:
  1. If a person really wants to continue working and his company really wants his special talents, there are usually special ways this can be handled.

2. If the company feels the employee is no longer able to function at full capacity and demands retirement, this will be more emotionally damaging to the person than mandatory age-based retirement.
3. Retirement is *wonderful* and it may be later than a workaholic thinks! (#59)

Our sample was management-oriented and this influenced their replies. A general feeling was that "industry needs young, willing, hard-working people."

Other comments concerning national policies centered around earned-income restrictions on Social Security payments. A Manufacturing retiree who spent 43 years in industrial relations makes the following calculation:

I am very upset currently with the Social Security change in the law to an annual earnings test (it has been monthly). This means that instead of losing only Social Security benefits in the months when I earn over $4000/12, on earnings of $14,000 I will lose all of my Social Security benefits. Since I will have to pay taxes (including the Social Security tax) on this $14,000, I only gain about $1000 per year more than if I earn $4000. This is *confiscatory*. I have written key legislators who agree.

From the consulting viewpoint—S.S. limitations make it difficult to sensibly take short assignments at high pay—which I planned to do and have done to now. I do not want to work a full half-year or more. My work doesn't take anyone's job but helps improve a business operation, and as I see it now I am stupid to work beyond $4000 earnings in one to one and a half months. (#170)

Another Manufacturing retiree earning $25,000, who retired at age 65 in 1971 after 40 years in research and development and is currently both self-employed and consulting, complains:

Self-employed retired persons frequently have a problem with the social security earned-income restrictions. In self-employment there are two social security rules that may limit your earnings: one is the number of hours worked per week and the other is the definition of "substantial services." The definition of substantial services is so vague that one never knows how it will be interpreted.

Last year, for example, I earned about $500 over the maximum allowed of $3240 for employed persons. I was definitely self-employed and had been working that way for several years. However, I was notified that I and my wife would lose nearly a month's social security because of the $500 and after I paid taxes plus self-employment tax of 7.9%, I lost $14 by earning that $500. In other words, the penalties and taxes were $514. (#39)

Social Security was viewed as an earned right, and there was some resentment that there was a ceiling on earnings but not on income from accumulated wealth. Because of these financial disincentives, some respondents claimed they would have otherwise considered work but were unwilling to take paid work, as this comment from a male Manufacturing retiree with a family income of $24,000, who retired three years ago at the age of 65 after 40 years in employee relations, relates:

The biggest disappointment of my retirement has been the Social Security restriction on earned income. It is most unfair and counterproductive. Having contributed to Social Security from its inception, the knowledge that I would have my benefits taken away from me if I did any significant work, made me rebel and decide *not* to do the consulting work that I was very well prepared to do and for which I had a potentially lucrative and professionally rewarding consulting agreement. It probably doesn't make sense to others that I would let such a "petty" factor influence my life—but I can say that my revolt "against the Social Security system" was and is very real and deep and soured me on carrying out my plans. (#455)

Unique Situations

A number of respondents faced situations or problems which were unique. These included the 69-year-old male Chain Store retiree who had twins two years before his retirement in 1972 and the female Utility retiree who married for the first time at the age of 56 to a man who lived 120 miles away, changing her retirement plans in order to be nearer to him:

I had been making plans to retire in 1976 when I attained 35 years' service and had expected to do volunteer work, travel and give travel lectures (illustrated), and perhaps do some part time work. My marriage changed all that, and I retired to a completely new and different life, in which I am most happy. I work frequently with my husband (office work and selling) but am not paid—it just keeps us together more of the time. Having married so late (age 56) there is much to make up for, thus my retirement is quite different from what it would have been had I remained single, or had I had a normal married life. (#662)

Unexpected health difficulties of the respondent or spouse also altered retirement plans in some instances. A male Manufacturing retiree with a family income of $9,000, who retired in 1972 at the age of 57 after 40 years in sales promotion and advertising management, writes:

One year after my retirement I suffered a major coronary and just managed to survive with severe heart damage. I had open heart surgery, had one-third of my heart removed. I am not an invalid but cannot do anything too strenuous or time-consuming.

I had planned on a good retirement with many shares of Chain Store stock to keep my wife and me going in our retirement. I had also planned on opening my own advertising agency to fill a void in time and earn additional income, but my heart attack canceled that plan. I am on Social Security disability which did limit any kind of part-time work. (#416)

Responsibilities toward parents or disabled children also affected the retirement of some respondents. One respondent writes:

I have great satisfaction in seeing our family business prosper with what seems to be a balanced leadership of all involved. I am president and accountant.

The move has worked out well for our retarded son, too, even though it did not work for him to live and learn from us as planned. (#361)

Another tells what he is doing with his time:

I am using the 40 hours I used to work in caring for my mother, who is 92 years old, and doing household chores. My wife is working part time. She is saving. I am dipping into my savings. It is possible I will work again. When I do I will prefer part-time work. It is possible I will sometime do voluntary work, if I have the time. We have continued to live in our home, which I repair and maintain. My mother lives with us. (#379)

7

Policy Implications

This study has concentrated on the postretirement experiences of a specific segment of the labor force, middle-level managerial and professional/technical personnel employed by large corporations. Moreover, it has been focused upon the postretirement work activities of individuals, the great majority of whom elected to retire or were forced to retire before reaching mandatory retirement age.

Early retirement is, along with the movement of women into the labor force, particularly married women, one of the major recent transformations of lifetime labor force experience. Our respondents retired, usually after some 30 to 40 years of employment by one firm, between 1968 and 1977. The pronounced trend toward early retirement, continual and rapid inflation, major changes in the legal and institutional framework within which retirement takes place, and, finally, significant transformations in the nature of the retirement experience itself, provide the framework for discussion of corporate or public policies which relate to the retirement experience of early retirees.

The study itself has confirmed our initial impression that for many early retirees, retirement does not conform to the all-or-nothing, the once-for-all decision and status that most people have in mind when they think of retirement. For a number of reasons—earlier age at retirement, longer life expectancy, better health, increased labor market options, better education, greater flexibility of working schedules, to name only some of the more important factors—a sizable proportion of our respondents indicated that they had significant and sustained labor market experience after their retirement from the corporation that had employed them for most of their life.

Moreover, the majority of these postretirement workers indicate that their labor market experiences after official retirement have been generally quite satisfactory. For many, postretirement employment experience has been the source of large, often extraordinary, financial and psychic rewards. And for an even larger proportion, postretirement employment has permitted the development of entirely new careers and interests.

At the same time, a significant proportion of our respondents indicate that labor market difficulties of one kind or another have forced them to accept less-than-satisfactory postretirement employment or no employment at all, in spite of a need or desire to work. Moreover, another sizeable group indicates that, although they have not worked during retirement, the pressures of inflation, compelling them to utilize savings and to liquidate other assets faster than they had anticipated, may force them to try to reenter the labor market. They face this prospect often with great trepidation and tend to believe that their age or the lengthy interruption of work experience will make it difficult or impossible for them to secure satisfactory employment.

Against this background, then, we will review some of the major policy issues that were outlined in the overview in the first chapter. These can be grouped around several problem areas. By far the most important problem is the effect of inflation upon postretirement standards of living. The policy responses can be grouped usefully into corporate, public and individual responses.

One corporate response to counter the effect of inflation upon pension benefits is to provide a limited cost-of-living adjustment (COLA). Corporate responses have commonly been ad hoc and episodic adjustments of pension benefits in the light of the inflationary erosion of their real value. But inflation has two quite distinct effects upon the situation of the retiree who is dependent upon pensions: one is the day-by-day erosion of his living standard produced by past inflation, the second is the uncertainty about the future value of his pension benefits. This uncertainty in some cases can be even more painful than actual decreases in living standards, particularly if an individual feels helpless in the face of it and contemplates the loss of all he has accumulated and an indefinite period of dependence on public or private charity.

Although it is clear that companies vary widely in their capacity to provide COLAs for pension benefits, it seems desirable for their pension policy to minimize wherever possible the uncertainties which pensioners feel about adjustments in pension benefits to inflation. Moreover, the retired feel that they should share in improvements in pension benefits that are received by the active labor force of a company.

Companies might consider the provision, particularly for middle-level managerial and professional/technical personnel, of a combination of pension plans which would make it possible for the individual to make voluntary contributions to increase his postretirement income. Since individuals differ in their need for postretirement income, they should have such options. Defined contribution benefit systems, such as those of TIAA/CREF, the major private provider of benefit plans for colleges and universities, often contain such options, of particular value to employees as they approach the retirement decision.

Benefit plans which would enable individuals to make voluntary contributions in the light of anticipated postretirement income needs should be coupled with improved information available to prospective retirees about their retirement income prospects, particularly as they may be affected by various levels of inflation and by age at retirement. Appropriate pension levels after retirement from one's primary lifetime employer are related to postretirement earning prospects. Improved information about employment opportunities go hand in hand with enlarged demand for part-time and part-year services of retirees.

Since home ownership has proved to be one of the most effective of inflation hedges, corporate and public policies which encourage the accumulation of equity in home ownership are desirable. A considerable proportion of early retirees relocate after retirement, but the majority remain in their homes. That portion of their lifetime savings which is embedded in the home is usually quite illiquid. The former employer might participate in financial arrangements which would enable homeowners to borrow easily and fully against the value of their home and help the retiree plan his expenditures rationally in the light of his total asset position. Since one characteristic of retirement is the necessity for sudden and potentially large expenditures for medical emergencies, any step which increases the liquidity of the retiree's portfolio of assets will contribute to the retiree's well-being and peace of mind. Here again a combination of public and corporate policies might be fruitful.

As pension benefit levels rise, a trend which has been given additional impetus by the recent agreements between General Motors and the UAW, the implicit bias against hiring older workers caused by differential pension costs by age is bound to increase the difficulties older workers face in securing reemployment after voluntary or involuntary retirement. Difficult as a solution to this very general problem may be, it is a necessary element in a program to improve the employment situation of older workers. We have emphasized throughout this volume that early retirement is not, and should not be considered to be, the same thing as permanent and complete retirement. Therefore the terms under which individuals who elect early retirement can secure reemployment, either full time or part time, become more and more a matter with which both public and corporate policy should be concerned.

The recent raising of the mandatory retirement age to 70 is probably only a way station on the road to elimination of all mandatory retirement. Already several states have taken this step. Although only a small proportion of individuals aged 70 or over are likely to be affected by the ending of all age-related mandatory retirement, corporate personnel policy must contend with the possibility that some older workers whose productivity has fallen substantially will want to continue working when they reach age 70.. Again this has particular relevance to the situation of early retirees who, .after a period of partial or complete retirement, find that they either want to go back to work or must, because of economic pressures and depleted assets, seek further employment. Facing an employment relationship open-ended with respect to age if they hire older workers, employers may well elect to avoid hiring them.

While age discrimination against presently employed older workers may be avoided by employers who fear litigation in which unions will take part, subtle forms of age discrimination in hiring may evolve. Such discrimination may be harder to prove and less likely to result in the discriminated-against individual attempting to secure redress from the courts.

Because of the raising of the legal mandatory retirement age to 70 and the probable abolition of any age-related mandatory retirement, in the near future corporate personnel policy must evolve new techniques and procedures to evaluate work performance. Dismissal of workers simply because of age, either directly or by means of procedures and techniques of evaluation which are thinly disguised substitutes for age discrimination, is not a feasible policy for large corporations over the long run. The immediate implication for personnel policy is that evaluation procedures and hiring criteria must become age neutral on the one hand, and effective on the other.

Since evaluations which lead to dismissal or denial of promotion can be, and will be, challenged in court, courts will require that evaluations, wherever possible, be objective and quantitative rather than qualitative. It will no longer be sufficient to assert that such and such a worker did an "excellent" job or that another worker has performed "poorly." The courts are certain to ask for clear-cut criteria of performance and adequate feedback arrangements between the evaluator and the worker being evaluated to permit the worker either to contest what he feels is an erroneous evaluation or, if it has a basis in fact, to take corrective steps within a reasonable period of time.

Similarly, dismissal because of productivity below a reasonable standard will depend, for long-service employees, upon records which document a history of declining productivity. If an older worker, dismissed because of allegations that his performance has fallen below minimum standards, can demonstrate that younger workers have not been dismissed, even though their performance in some cases has been no better, a charge of age discrimination is likely to be prima facie. Moreover, a worker who is confronted with declining performance evaluations should be provided an adequate opportunity to take corrective action. In the case of older workers, this might take the form of the employing institution arranging for transfer to less-demanding jobs or more-flexible hours.

This point takes on added bite when it is placed against the fact that one out of six of our respondents who initiated an early retirement did so because of reasons related to work pressures. In their written comments, a number of respondents added that these pressures had arisen suddenly. Since employers quite frequently make a practice of assigning young and inexperienced workers to relatively undemanding work tasks, a failure to make similar adjustments for older workers could be construed to be an example of age discrimination. Corporations will be required to demonstrate that their personnel policies make reasonable allowances for age-related differences in strength, endurance, adaptability, skill and experience.

Since the interaction between the utilization of older workers and the costs of early retirement create complex problems of personnel costs, large corporations are paying increased attention to the age distribution of their work force, not only company-wide but also by department and function. Even if companies may face severe restrictions in dismissing older workers because of ADEA (Age Discrimination in Employment Act), they may still retain a considerable control over the ports of entry.

In some companies, hiring has generally been at the lower skill levels with the expectation that a combination of on-the-job training and experience will lead to a staffing of most of the upper-level jobs. By adding ports of entry at higher skill levels, such companies can increase the average age of the work force. At the opposite end of the age spectrum, companies have some power to lower the average age of retirement through improving the relative attractiveness of pension benefits for those who select early retirement. In practice this means that pension benefits are not lowered actuarially for those who select early retirement. Not only does this induce some individuals to retire earlier than they ordinarily would have, but some of the early retirees will then reenter the labor market in the hopes of securing jobs which are comparable to the ones from which they retired.

With the likely improvement of early retirement benefits by some corporations designed to produce a lowered age distribution, there will be an increased supply of able executives in their mid- to late-fifties who are eager to take advantage of the opportunities for upward mobility which a change in employers may provide, and who are financially able to take the chance that they will find such employment because they can rely on the cushion of fairly substantial retirement benefits. This will occur when able middle-level managers find their careers blocked through no fault of their own but simply because of the narrowing of the executive pyramid near the top levels.

Corporations may therefore find it to their advantage to search actively for managerial talent in this age bracket. Rather than assuming that an executive in his fifties searching for a job is probably not a strong candidate for promotion, they may find that a significant portion of the executive job searchers who have elected early retirement are in fact very able and highly motivated. Our respondents have provided examples of extraordinary success in new careers.

Therefore, corporations will need to watch carefully for the effects of early retirement on the quality of their upper-level managerial pool. It is unlikely that the selective process involved in early retirement will be neutral with respect to managerial ability.

The emergence of a select group of middle-level managers who retire to take advantage of early retirement benefits but with the intention of finding new careers offers a potential windfall of managerial talent for alert corporations. Another group of early retirees and retirees who have retired at the normal retirement age may provide a valuable and flexible source of high-level ability and experience. These are the individuals who have retired but are eager or willing to act as consultants or to take advantage of part-time and part-year employment, either on a seasonal basis or at irregular intervals.

Corporations have long known how to use part-time personnel on relatively low-level tasks when the work load is highly irregular or varies on a weekly, monthly or seasonal basis. Many executive tasks vary in the same fashion, and the development of specialized management consultant and business service firms to provide temporary high-level talent is a feature of the recent past. The use by corporations of the middle- and upper-level managerial and professional talent possessed by their own retirees would often be of great benefit. Two reasons for using one's own retirees rather than calling upon outside management consulting firms or providers of business services are readily apparent. The first is that the retiree will usually be familiar with the standard operating procedures of the firm, with the personnel with whom he is working, and with the objectives and problems of the corporation. Secondly, the retiree is more apt to identify himself with the interests of his company and hence to preserve the confidentiality of matters which are private to the firm.

It would seem desirable for corporations to explore the possibility of creating a pool of retired managerial and professional/technical personnel interested in taking on specific assignments from the company or working for it on a regular, if still part-time and part-year, basis. A moderate retaining fee might even be in order to indicate that both sides of this new relationship take it seriously.

In the past the relationship between retiree and his company has often been characterized by a standoffish attitude, even to the extent of sometimes formally precluding any further utilization of the retiree by his company. This attitude towards the retiree was in the line with the belief that retirement status was, or should be, total and permanent and that it was not right for a retiree to receive any form of pension benefits unless he was entirely retired. Even so, many companies recognized the value of certain retired managerial and professional/technical personnel and would call upon them either routinely for advice or occasionally for assistance in crisis situations.

An employee approaching his sixties may prefer a reduction in working hours rather than early retirement and subsequent reemployment. A policy of permitting leaves of absence or significant reductions in hours worked or days worked per week would in some cases delay the retirement of valued talent. Since older managerial and professional/technical personnel are often their own most severe critics and are fully aware of declines in strength and ability which make it difficult to fulfill the most-demanding assignments, corporations should explore the possibility of using older managerial and professional/technical personnel who wish to continue working in less-demanding and less-prestigious jobs.

Although compulsory reassignment goes against the grain of most people, a reassignment which is voluntary and which permits the individual concerned to maintain his contact with the world of work is a different matter. Often an individual who has carried executive burdens for many years experiences profound relief when he no longer has to strain every nerve to fulfill his own and his company's expectations. Our respondents often gave fervent expression to this sense of relief and called attention to the satisfactions provided by jobs which utilized other capacities and strengths.

Full retirement has too often been the only respite for individuals who have long been under exhorbitant stress. Corporations should be able to find ways in which many individuals can retain a more flexible relationship with their company while preserving their dignity and permitting them to lay down as much of their burden as they wish.

Large corporations have always been confronted with the problem of reconciling the desires of the middle-level and higher-level managerial and professional/technical personnel, who are in the latter part of their careers (for stability of employment, retention or enhancement of status, and increased compensation) with the necessity that younger managerial and professional/technical personnel be offered advancement and recognition.

A constructive resolution of intergenerational conflicts over status depends, in part, upon whether older employees are offered adequate possibilities for shifts in careers, new status, and tapering-off of career. If large corporations acknowledge that older managerial and professional/technical personnel have extensive experience and multiple talents which it is in the interest of the corporation and the individual to utilize, but which require flexible and innovative personnel practices, then conflict between generations can be minimized and perhaps even replaced by cooperation and integration of efforts. On the other hand, older managerial employees will also have to be receptive to more flexible career patterns and innovative ways of utilizing the potentialities of older employees.

Only a few managerial personnel, approaching their sixties and their seventies, are apt to insist upon complete retention of all their status, power and compensation. Personnel practices of large corporations should be based, not upon those who are most rigid in asserting their positions or upon those whom increasing age has made least productive, but upon a sense of the diversity of older managerial personnel and the large potential they have for enhancing the firm's interests in the form of know-how, experience and dedication to the firm, all of which should be passed on to their successors as effectively and completely as possible.

The large corporation has in the recent past given a large part of the attention it devotes to its human resources to the intake of new members of its labor force—their training, retention and promotion. Customarily, it has paid much less attention to the effective utilization of employees during the years immediately preceding their retirement.

The treatment of managerial and professional/technical personnel who are approaching the time at which early retirement is feasible is certain to affect the morale of its entire staff and the firm's capacity to retain existing personnel and to attract new supplies of high-quality managerial talent. Short-run considerations may be at odds with long-run considerations, particularly when the subtle issues of firm morale and productivity are at stake. Here again the firm's policy, with respect to early retirement of its managerial personnel and their subsequent experiences, is bound to have important effects, even though often delayed and indirect. The "golden handshake," costly though it may be, may seem in fact to pay off in the short run. For a firm which is dependent upon recruiting the ablest members of the new generation of scientists and engineers, at a later date it may cost the firm the services of an exceptional individual without which it cannot survive.

Large corporations, confronted by the possibility that increased numbers of older managerial and professional/technical personnel may elect to stay with the firm until they reach significantly older ages than is presently the case, have an incentive to develop personnel practices which make effective use of the productive potential of older managerial personnel. In many firms there is all-too-little systematic knowledge upon which to base personnel policies. Yet firms often possess, in the persons of retired employees who have maintained a consultant relationship to the firm, a cadre of elderly employees who can offer some guidance and counsel to the firm about how to use older employees who want to continue to contribute but who at the same time are willing to exchange the formal constraints of the preretirement employment relationship for the looser tie of a consultant relationship.

The Interaction of Private Pensions and Social Security Benefits

Just as private pension systems with defined benefits are usually not age-neutral in their effects upon the supply of and the demand for labor, commonly creating incentives on the part of the employee to retire and on the part of the employer to dismiss or not hire older workers, so too does Social Security policy give older workers powerful incentives to retire before reaching mandatory retirement age and not to resume full-time work after they begin to draw Social Security benefits.

If it were public and private policy to foster early retirement, the design and operation of both public and private pension systems would be similar to what we now have in effect. Workers are encouraged to elect early retirement, while many older employees who want to keep on working encounter more severe difficulties when they seek reemployment after dismissal or, after a period of retirement, desire to resume paid employment.

The rapid increase in the number of older individuals who are receiving Social Security disability benefits may also indicate that, for an unknown number of persons, the eligibility criteria and benefit formulas of the disability provisions of Social Security act as an incentive to elect early retirement. This is not to say that their disabilities are unreal. Many substantial disabilities do not preclude working, however, and often the disabled individual is benefited by employment. The powerful drive to employ severly disabled younger workers is based upon the beneficial effects of employment upon their physical and psychological condition. What is true for the younger disabled person is often just as true for older people.

It is generally agreed that a reform of the disincentive effects of present Social Security benefit formulas cannot be secured by reducing present benefit levels or changing the nominal ages for eligibility. This does not mean that nothing can be done. Without reducing any present benefits, it will be possible for Congress to allocate the increases in future benefit levels in ways that will, over time, substantially reduce the disincentive effects of the Social Security system upon the work effort of older workers.

Raising or entirely eliminating the ceiling on earned income before reductions in benefits takes place is one step in this direction. A change of the formula for benefit reduction when the earned income ceiling is reached which would reduce the loss in benefits is another. Another change that could decrease the disincentive effects of Social Security would be substantial increases in the size of benefits for every additional year that an employee worked after age 65. Sufficiently large increases would make it possible to achieve some of the objectives that those who have advocated increasing the formal retirement age for full benefits from 65 to 68 have in mind.

Changing the incentive structure of private and public pension systems will not be costless. But what should be kept firmly in mind by policy-makers is the cost of doing nothing, the alternative. The trend toward early retirement has been one of the more massive social developments of the last few decades. It has already cost the nation large amounts in the form of the benefits paid to these early retirees and, just as economically significant, in the form of the decrease in the national output occasioned by their nonparticipation in the labor force.

The relative value of private and public pensions in a period of high inflation will alter rapidly and inexorably if the public pension is indexed against inflation and the private pension is not. Moreover, if the benefits payable to present employees are increased as part of the collective bargaining process (a likely result), the discrepancy between pensions paid to former employees who have been retired for some years and those held out to presently unretired employees may in many instances become quite large.

The erosion of the value of private pensions because of high rates of inflation may soon have, we believe, a pronounced effect upon the frequency and length of the period of early retirement. The comments of our respondents and the behavior of many of them during retirement are indications that high rates of inflation and uncertainty about the real value of pensions will decrease the willingness of managerial and professional/technical personnel to elect early retirement. This will be particularly the case if possibilities for salaried employment, consulting work or self-employment are relatively scarce for managerial and professional/technical personnel after they have elected early retirement.

Some Concluding Remarks

Public policy with respect to individuals who have elected early retirement and are in the retirement stage should recognize that a large number, if not a majority, are interested in either paid employment or in public service. The comments of our respondents about public service opportunities indicated that many of them felt that the major institutions which offer opportunities for voluntary service (churches, educational institutions, government and so forth) were often unaware of, unalert about, or uninterested in what retirees can offer in the way of specific and highly valuable skills.

Concerted action by governmental and nonprofit agencies can improve the linkages between these agencies and the retirees interested in public service or paid work. We have been impressed, however, with the extent to which our respondents relied upon the network of personal contacts and long-standing associations to secure either paid work or voluntary service. Most of them will probably continue to rely upon this kind of network.

Programs directed at utilizing the talents and efforts of retired managerial or professional/technical employees should be based upon a proper appreciation of the diversity of their interests, energies and ambitions. But they should also recognize the generally high levels of activity maintained by the retirees during most of their retirement years. With the exception of a very few individuals, most of whom have severe health problems, retirement is as far as can be imagined from the stereotypical image of the rocker on the porch.

That stereotype, very much of a rural character, may have been appropriate for an earlier day when the farmer would indeed rock away a few hours at the end of a hard day's work and more hours at the end of a hard lifetime's work. Instead our respondents demonstrated high levels of activity, myriads of interests, initiative and innovation, and a willingness and ability to explore all sorts of new options. These options included working or not working, voluntary service or tending one's own garden. Among the respondents were vigorous and eloquent spokesmen for the rewards and penalties of each of these ways of using the time afforded by early retirement.

We started our investigation because we were concerned about whether early retirement might have led to a widespread waste of a valuable national resource: the skills, energies and experience of managerial and professional/technical personnel. Based upon the

experiences of the respondents from the three large national corporations who provided us with data, along with numerous comments
upon public and private issues, a considerable proportion of the early
retirees who were managers or professional/technical personnel are
able to make very full and productive use of their postretirement
years.

But that is not the whole story. A minority, vocal and often quite
bitter, believe that their talents and abilities are not being properly
utilized, that either their former corporation or the nation at large, or
both, are insensitive to their needs, unappreciative of their services,
and neglectful of their potential contribution.

Private and public policy should focus attention upon this group.
One aim of policy should be to address their immediate concerns. A
more fundamental aim would be to decrease their numbers in the
future.

APPENDIX

The Questionnaire

Our survey instrument is reproduced below. Several types of data were requested. The first and eighth parts of the questionnaire were designed to elicit information on time allocated to various activities in the past year and, for comparative purposes, in the year before retirement. These activities included types of paid work, hobbies, and recreational pursuits. Other parts of the questionnaire focused on postretirement work experience either in salaried employment for a company, self-employment, or consulting. There were additional sections concerned with volunteer work, the retirement decision and the planning process that accompanied it, financial information, geographical mobility, satisfaction, and basic demographic data.

A final section of the questionnaire left room for open-ended comments and/or recommendations, particularly those on the subjects of postretirement employment, company pension and retirement policies and national policies with respect to retirement, age discrimination and social security. About one-third of the respondents made comments in the end section. Although not all individuals wrote on all the requested topics, most comments were limited to the topics suggested. A number added additional exhibits, photographs, and personal information to their questionnaires.

The Sample: A General View

The survey questionnaire for the Retirement Activities Study was sent out in the spring of 1978. Our sample consisted of 1,550 retirees. Six hundred were from the Manufacturer, 450 from the Chain Store, and 500 from the Utility. Of these, 1,045 individuals responded, a response rate of 67 percent. Return rates for each corporation differed slightly: 70 percent (N=420) for the Manufacturer, 65 percent (N=292) for the Chain Store and 60 percent (N=299) for the Utility.* These return rates were greater than those generally anticipated for mailed questionnaires. Many respondents appeared highly motivated to respond to the survey, noting that they found the questionnaire quite relevant to their present condition as retirees.

The average salary of our respondents at retirement was $28,800 (in 1977 dollars). Sixty-two percent of our respondents had been managers, and 38 percent had been either technical or professional workers before retirement. The youngest early retiree among our respondents had retired at the age of 46. Most of the early retirees, however, had retired in their early 60s.

Although we had hoped to find more women among middle-level management and technical/professional employees, almost all of our respondents were male (95 percent). Seventy percent were the sole breadwinners for their family in the year before retirement. About 95 percent were married when they retired, and over 90 percent were currently married, most with spouses between the ages of 60 and 68 years, although 2 percent had spouses 50 years of age or less.

Our respondents were well educated for their age group. Twenty-two percent were college graduates but had done no graduate work. Twenty percent had education beyond an undergraduate degree. Another 34 percent had had some college education but had not graduated. About one-quarter of our respondents had no college experience.

Differences Among Respondents
from the Three Corporations

The respondents from the Chain Store and the Utility were more likely to retire in their 50s than were those from the Manufacturer (26

*3.3 percent (N=34) of the respondents did not indicate their preretirement corporate affiliation.

percent and 27 percent respectively compared with 12 percent). A higher percentage of the Chain Store respondents retired in their early 60s (39 percent compared to 33 percent for the Manufacturer and 32 percent for the Utility, no doubt in part as a result of the Chain Store's earlier mandatory retirement policy for part of the period 1968-1977 (63 years of age compared with 65). A higher proportion of the Utility respondents were early retirees (79 percent compared to 73 percent in both other companies), but this may be more a reflection of corporate differences in sampling and response rates rather than actual differences in the proportions electing early retirement within all three corporations.

COLUMBIA UNIVERSITY

Conservation Of Human Resources Project

Retirement Activities Study

All information in this questionnaire is CONFIDENTIAL

TO MAIL: FOLD OVER FLAP OF BACK COVER, SEAL, AND POST.

I. First we would like to know how you usually divided your time among some specific activities.

1. Approximately how many hours per week did you devote to these activities in a typical week (A) in the year just before your retirement and (B) in the past 12 months?

Activities	(A) Hours spent per week in the year just before retirement	(B) Hours spent per week in the past 12 months
Salaried employment (do not include travel time)	_____	_____
Other paid work (e.g. self-employment, do not include travel time)	_____	_____
Volunteer work (e.g. civic, political, religious)	_____	_____
Hobbies & recreation	_____	_____
Routine domestic chores	_____	_____
Home maintenance and improvement (e.g. painting, carpentering, etc.)	_____	_____

2. How much did the pattern of hours you indicated in column B vary during the course of the year?

    a. A great deal ☐
    b. Moderately ☐
    c. Little or not at all ☐

3. If your answer to question 2 was (a) or (b), what caused the variation?
    (Check all appropriate boxes)

    a. Illness ☐
    b. Travel ☐
    c. Changes in my employment schedule ☐
    d. Seasonal recreation ☐
    e. Other (please specify) _____

4. During most of the months since your retirement, have you been engaged in salaried employment, consulting work, self-employment, or actively looked for income-producing activity?

    a. Yes ☐
    b. No ☐

II. Have you worked for an employer since retirement in a capacity other than consulting?

Yes ☐   No ☐ If No, please go to section III.

If Yes, please answer the following questions for (A) your present or most recent job and (B) your longest held job after retirement *other* than your present or most recent job.

	(A) Present or Most Recent Job	(B) Longest Held Job Since Retirement Other than Your Present or Most Recent Job
		Have not had more than one post-retirement job ☐

Please indicate in the spaces provided,

1. number of months you
    worked for this employer
    since retirement   _____   _____

Please put a check in the appropriate boxes,

2. Size of firm
    a. under 100 employees   ☐   ☐
    b. 100 to 499 employees   ☐   ☐
    c. 500 or more employees   ☐   ☐

3. Compared to your last
    job before retirement,
    was this work
    a. very much the same   ☐   ☐
    b. somewhat similar   ☐   ☐
    c. quite different   ☐   ☐

4. Which of the following best
    characterized your working time?
    a. Part time, part of the year   ☐   ☐
    b. Full time, part of the year   ☐   ☐
    c. Part time, full year   ☐   ☐
    d. Full time, full year   ☐   ☐

	(A) Present or Most Recent Job	(B) Longest Held Job Since Retirement Other than Your Present or Most Recent Job

5. Which of the following patterns of working time would you have preferred?

	(A)	(B)
a. Part time, part of the year	☐	☐
b. Full time, part of the year	☐	☐
c. Part time, full year	☐	☐
d. Full time, full year	☐	☐

6. How did you obtain this job?

	(A)	(B)
a. Personal contact	☐	☐
b. Employment agency	☐	☐
c. Response to employer's ad	☐	☐
d. Assistance from company I worked for before retirement	☐	☐
e. Other (please specify)	_____	_____

7. How long did you look for this job?

	(A)	(B)
a. I had already made arrangements for this job before retirement	☐	☐
b. less than a month	☐	☐
c. between 1 and 6 months	☐	☐
d. more than 6 months	☐	☐

8. Why did you go back to work? (Check all applicable boxes)

	(A)	(B)
a. I wanted more income for my spouse and myself	☐	☐
b. I wanted the income to help contribute to the support of my children	☐	☐
c. I was very concerned about the effect of inflation upon my future standard of living	☐	☐
d. I wanted more contact with people	☐	☐
e. Taken as a whole, I liked to keep working	☐	☐
f. I was concerned that not working would have an adverse effect on my health	☐	☐
g. Other (please specify)	_____	_____

9. Compared to my pre-retirement job, this work was

	(A)	(B)
a. much more satisfying	☐	☐
b. somewhat more satisfying	☐	☐
c. about the same	☐	☐
d. somewhat less satisfying	☐	☐
e. much less satisfying	☐	☐

III. Have you been self-employed and/or acted as a consultant since retirement?

Yes ☐   No ☐ If No, please go to Section IV.

If Yes, please answer the following questions:

1. Which of the following would describe your activities?

☐ self-employment   ☐ consulting work

128

2. If you are *presently* self-employed and/or acting as a consultant, please check appropriate box(es)

☐ self-employment   ☐ consulting work

3. Which of the following best characterizes your working time in your present (or most recent) self-employment or consulting activity?
   a. Part time, part of the year ☐
   b. Full time, part of the year ☐
   c. Part time, full year ☐
   d. Full time, full year ☐

4. Compared to my pre-retirement job, this work was (is)

	Self-employment	Consulting
a. much more satisfying	☐	☐
b. somewhat more satisfying	☐	☐
c. about the same	☐	☐
d. somewhat less satisfying	☐	☐
e. much less satisfying	☐	☐

5. What are the reasons why you took this work? *(Check all applicable boxes)*

	Self-employment	Consulting
a. I wanted more income for my spouse and myself	☐	☐
b. I wanted the income to help contribute to the support of my children	☐	☐
c. I was very concerned about the effect of inflation upon my future standard of living	☐	☐
d. I wanted more contact with people	☐	☐
e. Taken as a whole, I liked to keep working	☐	☐
f. I was concerned that not working would have an adverse effect on my health	☐	☐
g. Other (please specify)	_____	_____

6. I am self-employed and/or engage in consulting work because *(Check all applicable boxes)*:
   a. I always have wanted to engage in this type of activity ☐
   b. I can earn more this way than by working for an employer ☐
   c. I wanted to work but could find no opportunities to work for an employer ☐
   d. It gives me more flexibility in hours than work for an employer ☐
   e. If I establish myself in self-employment or in consulting work, I will be able to work as many more years as I choose ☐
   f. Other (please specify) _____

IV. If you have not worked for pay at all during the last twelve months, please answer the following questions.

1. What are the reasons why you are no longer working?
   (Check all applicable boxes)
   a. There are no post-retirement job opportunities in my former field ☐
   b. There are no post-retirement job opportunities in any field ☐
   c. My health does not permit it ☐
   d. After taxes and other deductions, including social security, the incentive to work is not sufficient ☐
   e. I do not want to work anymore ☐
   f. Other (please specify) _____

2. If you are not working, but interested in employment, which of the following work schedules would you prefer?
   a. Full time for the full year ☐   c. Part time for the full year ☐
   b. Full time for part of the year ☐   d. Part time for part of the year ☐

129

V. Have you done volunteer work in (A) the year just before your retirement and/or (B) the past 12 months?

Yes ☐   No ☐ If No, please go to Section VI.

If Yes, please answer the following questions:

	(A) Year Just Before Retirement	(B) Past 12 months
1. Has your volunteer work been primarily for		
a. Religious organizations	☐	☐
b. Health and social welfare agencies	☐	☐
c. Political organizations	☐	☐
d. Business advisory services (e.g. minority businesses)	☐	☐
e. Other (please specify)	_____	_____
2. How would you characterize your pattern of volunteer work?		
a. I would have liked to have spent more time in volunteer work	☐	☐
b. I spent as much time as I would have liked in volunteer work	☐	☐
c. I would have liked to have spent less time in volunteer work	☐	☐
3. How was this volunteer work related to the kind of work you did for your pre-retirement employer?		
a. Very closely related	☐	☐
b. Somewhat related	☐	☐
c. Not at all related	☐	☐

VI. We would now like to ask you some questions about your decision to retire and the planning that accompanied it. We realize that it is sometimes difficult to recall exactly what you either thought or did several years ago, but in order for your answer to be most useful, it would be helpful to us for you to try to recall as much as you can about your thoughts and actions before you retired. For several different areas in which planning might occur, we would like for you to indicate whether you (A) made no plans at all, (B) thought about the subject, (C) took some concrete steps to carry out your plans. For example, if you thought before retirement about moving to Florida, check (B). If you consulted real estate brokers either to sell your home or to purchase a new residence, check (C).

	(A) No Plans	(B) Thought About the Subject	(C) Took Concrete Steps
1. Planning for:			
a. salaried employment after retirement	☐	☐	☐
b. self-employment or consulting work	☐	☐	☐
c. spouse's retirement	☐	☐	☐
d. post-retirement income from investments	☐	☐	☐
e. travel	☐	☐	☐
f. change of residence	☐	☐	☐

    check applicable box(es) if you planned to move to
    a) a retirement community ☐   b) the sunbelt ☐

2. If you answered (B) or (C) in question 1, in which of the following areas did your planning help you adjust to the reality of retirement?

	planning very useful	planning somewhat useful	planning not at all useful
a. salaried employment after retirement	☐	☐	☐
b. self-employment or consulting work	☐	☐	☐
c. spouse's retirement	☐	☐	☐
d. post-retirement income from investments	☐	☐	☐
e. travel	☐	☐	☐
f. change of residence	☐	☐	☐

3. At the time you retired, what did you estimate the average rate of inflation would be during your retirement?
   a. Under 5% ☐
   b. 5% or more ☐
   c. At the time I retired, I do not recall giving much thought to it. ☐

4. Did you use any company-provided counselling resources to assist you in planning for your retirement?
   a. Yes ☐   b. No ☐
   If Yes,   If No,
   a. I found them very useful ☐   a. My company did not provide them ☐
   b. I found them only   b. My company provided them, but I
      moderately useful ☐   did not think they would be useful ☐
   c. I found them of little   c. My company provided them, but I
      or no use ☐   did not wish to discuss my per-
                                            sonal situation with company-
                                            provided retirement counselors ☐

5. How long before your retirement, did you feel that you knew in which year you would retire?
   a. I did not know when I would retire ☐
   b. In the year before I actually retired ☐
   c. More than a year before ☐

6. Did you initiate a request for retirement?
   a. Yes ☐
   b. No ☐

7. If you initiated a request for retirement, was it based upon any of the following circumstances? (Check all applicable boxes)
   a. I finally had enough assets to make it possible to retire ☐
   b. An attractive pension offer was made ☐
   c. I received an attractive job offer from another employer ☐
   d. The time was opportune for me to engage in consulting work or self-employment ☐
   e. Concern for my health made it desirable to retire when I did ☐
   f. The physical demands of my job were becoming too great ☐
   g. The stresses of making decisions and solving problems were becoming excessive ☐
   h. It was becoming more and more difficult for me to live up to my company's performance expectations ☐
   i. Having risen as far as I could within the firm, my job no longer provided the same challenge and satisfaction ☐
   j. I found myself less and less content to work under supervision ☐
   k. A conflict with my superiors made retirement desirable ☐
   l. I felt that I had worked long enough for my company ☐
   m. After taxes, the incentive to continue working was no longer sufficient ☐
   n. Other (please specify) _____

8. If you did not initiate a request for retirement, was your retirement based upon any of the following circumstances? *(Check all applicable boxes)*
   a. There was a company-wide reduction in personnel ☐
   b. There was a reduction in personnel in my own division or department ☐
   c. The company gave me an option which I was glad to take ☐
   d. There was a conflict with my superiors ☐
   e. I had reached mandatory retirement age ☐
   f. Other (please specify) _____

9. Did the company you retired from place any restrictions upon your subsequent employment?
   a. Yes, I could not work for related companies ☐
   b. Yes, I could not do consulting work for my company ☐
   c. No ☐
   d. Other (please specify) _____

10. In retrospect, all things considered, do you feel that you retired
    a. too soon ☐
    b. at about the right time ☐
    c. too late ☐

11. If you feel that you retired too soon, which of the following are reasons why you feel this way? *(Check all applicable boxes)*
    a. The behavior of the stock market has adversely affected my net worth, causing me to worry about my standard of living ☐
    b. Inflation has eroded the value of my income ☐
    c. I don't have enough to do with my time ☐
    d. I miss the contact with people I had on my job ☐
    e. I miss the challenge and excitement involved in performing successfully on my job ☐
    f. Other (please specify) _____

12. If you feel that you retired too late, which of the following are reasons why you feel this way? *(Check all applicable boxes)*
    a. I enjoy being free from pressures related to my job before retirement and wish I had freed myself sooner ☐
    b. Remaining too long with the job I had before retirement adversely affected my health ☐
    c. I would have been able to carry out some of the plans I had for retirement which my health now prevents me from doing ☐
    d. If I had retired earlier, I would have been able to secure better post-retirement work ☐
    e. Other (please specify) _____

13. Taken as a whole, how would you characterize your experiences during retirement?
    a. Very much what I expected ☐
    b. Fairly similar to what I expected ☐
    c. Only partially what I expected ☐
    d. Not at all what I expected ☐

14. If you checked (c) or (d) in question 13, which of the following were reasons why your expectations were not met? *(Check all appropriate boxes)*
    a. Fewer health problems (including problems of spouse) than I expected after retirement ☐
    b. More health problems (including problems of spouse) than I expected after retirement ☐
    c. Income after retirement higher than I anticipated ☐
    d. Income after retirement has limited activities more than I anticipated ☐
    e. My social life has been more satisfying than I expected ☐
    f. My social life has been less satisfying than I expected ☐
    g. Other (please specify) _____

VII. We would now like to ask you some questions about your finances. We know it is difficult to be precise in these matters and have therefore provided you with broad categories in most cases. We would like to remind you that all information in this questionnaire is anonymous and confidential. We would first like to ask you some questions about *your earnings* and the *earnings of your spouse from employment:*

1. What was your total annual salary from employment at your company in the year before your retirement to the nearest thousand dollars (be sure to include bonuses and/or merit payments):

   _____

2. Approximately what percentage of your family's total annual earned income was contributed by your own earnings from salaried employment and/or self-employment (be sure *not* to include your spouse's earnings, your pension or social security in calculating your own earnings).

	(A) Year Just Before Retirement	(B) Past 12 Months
a. None — I did not have any earnings		☐
b. 25% or less	☐	☐
c. 26-50%	☐	☐
d. 51-75%	☐	☐
e. 76% or more	☐	☐
f. All of it. My spouse was not gainfully employed	☐	☐

Now we would like to ask you some questions about your *total family income:*

	(A) Year Just Before retirement	(B) Past 12 Months
3. What was your total family income from all sources to the nearest thousand dollars?	_____	_____
4. Approximately what percentage of your total family income from all sources came from your or your spouse's investments?		
a. 25% or less	☐	☐
b. 26-50%	☐	☐
c. 51-75%	☐	☐
d. 76% and over	☐	☐
5. Approximately what percentage of your total family income from all sources came from your retirement pension and social security?		
a. 25% or less		☐
b. 26-50%		☐
c. 51-75%		☐
d. 76% and over		☐

6. Have you deferred receiving your
   a. pension from your company? Yes ☐ No ☐
   b. social security retirement payments? Yes ☐ No ☐

VIII. We would now like to ask you some questions about the kinds of activities you engaged in and how you used your time. For each of the following activities indicate whether you engaged in them (a) frequently, (b) occasionally, or (c) rarely or never (A) in the year just before retirement and (B) in the past twelve months by placing a check in the apropriate boxes. (We realize that some of these activities are seasonal in character. For seasonal activities, please use the season, rather than the year, as your frame of reference.)

	(A) In the year just before retirement			(B) In the past 12 months		
	(a) Frequently	(b) Occasionally	(c) Rarely or never	(a) Frequently	(b) Occasionally	(c) Rarely or never
1. Active sports (e.g. tennis, golf, jogging, hiking, etc.)	☐	☐	☐	☐	☐	☐
2. General household repair	☐	☐	☐	☐	☐	☐
3. Gardening	☐	☐	☐	☐	☐	☐
4. Travel	☐	☐	☐	☐	☐	☐
5. Theatre, concerts, movies and museums	☐	☐	☐	☐	☐	☐
6. Attending sports events	☐	☐	☐	☐	☐	☐
7. Bridge and other card games	☐	☐	☐	☐	☐	☐
8. Television	☐	☐	☐	☐	☐	☐
9. Arts and Crafts:						
Painting and sculpture	☐	☐	☐	☐	☐	☐
Music	☐	☐	☐	☐	☐	☐
Woodworking	☐	☐	☐	☐	☐	☐
Photography	☐	☐	☐	☐	☐	☐
Other arts and crafts	☐	☐	☐	☐	☐	☐
10. Reading:						
Newspapers and magazines	☐	☐	☐	☐	☐	☐
Current fiction	☐	☐	☐	☐	☐	☐
Literary classics	☐	☐	☐	☐	☐	☐
General nonfiction	☐	☐	☐	☐	☐	☐
Technical or business related material	☐	☐	☐	☐	☐	☐
11. Adult education courses	☐	☐	☐	☐	☐	☐

IX. Please provide the following additional information about yourself to complete our questionnaire:

1. Which of the following statements best applies to you?
   a. I now live more than a thousand miles from the community in which I lived right before my retirement ☐
   b. I have moved since retirement but live less than twenty miles from the community in which I lived right before my retirement ☐
   c. I live in the same house or apartment I lived in right before my retirement ☐
   d. Other (please specify present distance from community in which you lived right before retirement) _____

2. In what year did you retire? _____

3. How old were you at the time of your retirement? _____

4. What company were you employed by
   when you retired?
   a. General Electric ☐
   b. Sears Roebuck ☐
   c. AT&T ☐

5. How many years did you
   work for this company? _____

6. Sex
   a. Male ☐
   b. Female ☐

7. Marital Status: At time you·retired   At present
   a. Married   ☐   ☐
   b. Divorced or separated   ☐   ☐
   c. Single   ☐   ☐
   d. Widowed   ☐   ☐

8. If married, how old is your spouse? _____

9. Would you describe your job as   Before retirement   At present
   primarily: (if earning income)
   a. Managerial   ☐   ☐
   b. Technical/professional   ☐   ☐

10. Before retirement, would you describe your activities as primarily involved with
    a. Research and development ☐
    b. Production ☐
    c. Sales and marketing ☐
    d. Other (specify)_____

11. Years of education you have completed (check applicable box):
    a. High school graduate ☐
    b. Some college ☐
    c. College graduate ☐
    d. Some post-graduate ☐
    e. Graduate or professional degree ☐

12. Taking all things into consideration, how would you characterize your retirement?
    a. I am very satisfied ☐
    b. I am moderately satisfied ☐
    c. I am moderately dissatisfied ☐
    d. I am very dissatisfied ☐

13. Which of the following best describes your health since retirement?
    a. My health has improved since I retired ☐
    b. My health is about the same as it was just before I retired ☐
    c. My health has become worse since I retired ☐

14. Which of the following best describes your social life since retirement?
    a. I have a more active social life since I retired ☐
    b. My social life has remained about the same as it was just before I retired ☐
    c. I have a less active social life since I retired ☐

15. Have you joined any associations of retired persons?
    a. Yes ☐
    b. No ☐

16. If Yes, what was the primary reason you joined?
    a. I felt that retired people ought to have a stronger voice   ☐
    b. I wanted to take advantage of the financial benefits offered
       (e.g. discounts, insurance, group travel)   ☐
    c. I wanted to receive their publications   ☐
    d. The association offered the opportunity for desirable social contacts   ☐
    e. Other (please specify) _____

X. A questionnaire does not allow full expression of the diversity of individual experience and thoughts. If, in light of your retirement experience and your reflections thereon, you would like to make comments or recommendations about 1) post-retirement employment, including problems of age discrimination, 2) company pension or retirement policies, or 3) national policies with respect to retirement, age discrimination, and social security (e.g. social security earned-income restrictions) please use the space provided below and attach additional sheets if necessary. Do not feel constrained to the subjects we have listed. We are also very much interested in any other comments or recommendations you would like to make.

Index

About the Authors

Dean W. Morse is senior research associate, Conservation of Human Resources, Columbia University. He is the author of *The Peripheral Worker* and *Pride against Prejudice: Work in the Lives of Older Blacks and Young Puerto Ricans* and coauthor of *The Labor Market: An Information System* and *Comparative Metropolitan Employment Complexes: New York, Chicago, Los Angeles, Houston and Atlanta.*

Susan H. Gray has been a research associate at the Conservation of Human Resources, Columbia University, and is currently assistant professor of sociology at Fordham University. She has published several articles in the areas of social psychology, work and voluntary unemployment, and race relations.